JACK'S L

The Life of a Westmorland Agricultural Contractor 1953–2000

~

Bill Moffat

Compiled by Anne Bonney

HELM
PRESS

Dedicated to my wife and family

Published by Helm Press
10 Abbey Gardens, Natland, Kendal, Cumbria LA9 7SP

Tel: 015395 61321

E.mail: HelmPress@natland.freeserve.co.uk

Copyright – Bill Moffat and Anne Bonney

First published 2004

ISBN 0 9540497 7 2

Typeset and printed by
MTP Media Ltd, The Sidings, Beezon Fields, Kendal. Cumbria LA9 6BL

Front Cover
Top: Bill combining at Ninezergh Farm, Levens in 1960s.
Left: Harry Lancaster and his sons thatching at Low Sizergh Farm 1940s.
Centre: Break during harvesting at Low Longmire Farm in 1946.
Right: Dickie Mitchell at Crosthwaite Smithy 1965.

Contents

Bill with his recently restored 1963 Fordson Super Dexta tractor in Natland.

Introduction

I WAS BORN AND BROUGHT UP IN KENDAL and my father worked mainly in agriculture. He had a love of machinery and this was passed on to me and from an early age I helped him whatever he was doing. I was 'Jack's Lad' no less!

I had a good up bringing in Kendal, with my mum and dad and two sisters. Kendal was different then and children had relative freedom to run and play wherever they liked. We still had the canal and that was just literally round the back of our house and during hard winters we would skate on it. Life was relatively simpler then, you went to school, did your schooling and left and got a job. By the time I was due to leave dad had become his own boss and set up as an agricultural contractor. I must add that during the last few years of school I had been helping him more and more. I learned to drive the tractor and I became more and more useful to him. I helped to begin with after school or weekends but if he was busy and he wanted me I would just stay off school – so perhaps I did not get all the schooling I should have done. This of course was not uncommon then.

I joined him in the business – we moved out to Natland and built our own bungalow and sheds to house the growing business. As we became more established and got more work, we had to take on workers. I later married and had a daughter. Through time I lost both my mother and father but continued with the business on my own employing staff. It had its ups and downs but happily continued until 2000 when because of ill health I was advised to stop and I did so. I sadly sold of all my equipment.

I now live happily in another bungalow that we built just next to our original one and enjoy my retirement. I still do bits and pieces together with doing up farm machinery and visit the many friends that I made and who when passing often drop in to see me in my workshop.

This book would never have been written without the help of Anne Bonney and Mavis my wife. I am no hand at writing but with the help of Anne and Mavis this book has been put together. I would also like to take the opportunity to thank all the people that have assisted me with photographs, particularly Percy Duff who generously loaned us some of his pictures from his late wife Margaret's collection. Debts of gratitude to many friends, particularly Dennis Moorhouse who has also helped to jog my memory of the things that has happened during my life – it has been a hard one, with long hours but one that I would not have changed. It is a way of life that many will recognise and will not be dissimilar to their own, out in all weathers, often getting wet and bedraggled, missed mealtimes – a race against time to finish a job before the weather changed. So read on and enjoy and perhaps take yourself back in time!

Bill Moffat

March 2004

I

My Family

I WAS BORN WILLIAM JACKSON MOFFAT (BILL) in Kendal on 2 June 1938 and my father was John (Jack) William Moffat from Greenwood Hall Farm, Dent. My mother was called Bertha Ann, nee Mounsey, and originally came from Oaks Farm, Skelwith Bridge, Ambleside.

When I was born we lived at 'Scarbrook,' 76 Natland Road, Kendal. I was one of three, I had two sisters, Audrey being the oldest born in 1936, and then me in the middle and my younger sister Elizabeth (Libby), born in 1940.

My mother worked in her uncle's (Fleming Mawson's) general store, at Elterwater, for a few years before she married. My grandfather, Jackson Mounsey, and grandmother, Ann, farmed at Oaks Farm, just off Red Bank Road, the little side road that cuts through to Grasmere. This was a large hill farm that backed onto Loughrigg with the tarn behind. My mother was the youngest of five children. She had two brothers and two sisters, Harry, Jack, Dorothy and Sue. Grandmother was about forty when my mother was born and there was a large gap between my mother and the rest of the family.

Grandfather kept Herdwick sheep and in October every year they would take the sheep to be wintered at Wilson House Farm, Lindale, near Grange. They walked the sheep in those days from Oaks Farm, the three of them with three or four sheep dogs. There would be my Uncle Harry, grandfather and my great uncle. They would go down to Bowness, just walking them along the road, as there was little traffic in the 1920s. I remember them saying that they stayed at the Plough Inn and the sheep were penned up for the night in a paddock. (This was knocked down in 1923 and the Lyth Valley Hotel was built opposite).

The following morning they would take the sheep over Whitbarrow and come out at Rawsons Farm, near the quarry, and then out onto the main Witherslack road (now the A590) and onto Wilson House Farm, which was owned by my mother's uncle, Frank Atkinson. They took a lot of sheep. This took about two days in all and it was quite common to do this.

My father, John William Moffat on my grandmother's Elizabeth Moffat's knee.

My grandparents, Jackson Mounsey's farm sale in 1936 — Oaks Farm, Skelwith Bridge, Ambleside.

Wilson House was a two hundred and fifty acre arable farm and grew quite a lot of corn. It also had plenty of grass and stubble for wintering the sheep on. This was normal for hill farmers to winter sheep on low lying arable farms where there was plenty of grass and food for winter-feed through the winter months and take them back home again in the spring.

My grandfather, grandmother and my mother would go down afterwards to the farm with a horse and cart and pick up the strays and take them home. They usually made a day of it stopping for tea and catching up with news before returning home with the strays tied in the back of the cart.

My father, Jack was born in 1911 at Greenwood Haw Farm, Dent. The farm was on the main road between Sedbergh and Dent. He was one of seven. There was Daisy; Thomas (Tommy) the youngest; George; Louise; Joe and Violet (Vi). They also had another farm, Rash Farm that lay about a mile away. Greenwood Haw was the largest of the two, and stocked both Shorthorn cows that they milked and Swaledale sheep. They milked about twelve to fourteen and the milk was picked up from the wooden milk stand. They also kept a pig and some hens for the house.

As well as being a farmer Grandfather George Moffat was also a Methodist preacher and used to preach at nearby Rash Mill. Grandfather died when my father was only twelve. Grandma Elizabeth Moffat had to run both farms, she would work outside and Auntie Daisy would work inside looking after the children and doing the housework. Uncle Joe called her 'Pastry' because she was always making pasties. Everybody had to help out doing jobs. A few years later my grandmother managed to afford to employ Robert (Bob) Armistead as farm manager and they later married.

Father told me that when Uncle George and him used to walk the three miles over the top to the National School at Sedbergh, they would sometimes get into mischief along the way. The road lengths-men in those days were employed by the Council to keep a stretch of roadway. He had the responsibility of scything the grass on the roadside verges and keeping the gutters clean, thereby taking the water of the road. The road lengths-man that covered the area mentioned in those days had an old motorbike that he used to leave in the barn, at Dairy Farm, which was next to Rash Farm. Sometimes my father and uncle would nip into the barn and have a ride on the motorbike unbeknown to the poor lengths-man and he would be none the wiser. It was all a bit of harmless fun!

Rash Farm, near Sedbergh where my dad's parents lived. Dad is standing on the wall and grandma is on the left of the porch and granddad on the right wearing a flat cap.

My father, who was always known as Jack, left home when he was about fifteen years old and went into farm service. He worked at various farms including Elm Tree and Black Yeat at Preston Patrick, with Harry Howarth, from Gatebeck, who is sadly no longer with us.

Jack later went to work in a milk house belonging to my great uncle in Liverpool. A milk house was simply a dairy in the middle of the town. The cows sadly never saw the light of day. They were milked and fed inside. The milk houses were beautifully tiled and the milk was sold direct to the customers. This would be in the 1930s and I think he lived in. He stayed there for a short time before coming back up north.

Father then started working as a builder and stayed with his sister, Auntie Daisy, at a house called 'Riverside', at Sedgwick, where she reared pigs on the two acres of land they had, with her husband Roy Cooper, who was a local builder. In the 1930s they helped to build Kirkbarrow Estate, Kendal. My aunt and uncle eventually built a bungalow where the piggeries were and moved from Riverside into it. A few years ago the bungalow was knocked down and a large limestone house was built in its place.

My mother and father had met through motorcycling. My father and Uncle George had gone to buy a motorcycle from Peter MacDiarmid, who at that time was a gamekeeper at Barbon Manor and he was going out with Winnie Pepper, from Skelwith Bridge, Ambleside, who was mother's niece. Winnie and mother were great friends and spent a lot of time together and they were more like sisters and this is how they met up.

Uncle George and Peter McDiarmid outside 'Scarbrook', Natland Road, Kendal.

Some of the workers that helped to build Kirkbarrow Estate in Kendal in the 1930s. Dad is in the second row on the right and Uncle Roy is on the far left.

They would go out as a foursome to dances, motorcycling and skating. It was quite common in those days to go skating on Windermere when the lake was frozen. Both couples duly married. Father and mother were married at Brathay Church, Ambleside on 30 October 1935 and held their reception at the Skelwith Bridge Hotel and honeymooned in Blackpool before setting up house in Natland Road, Kendal.

In about 1937–38 he started working for Crofts, agricultural engineers, in Wildman Street, Kendal. They also had a depot at Ulverston and my father went there as a tractor driver and ploughman. He told me about when he was ploughing at Ireleth, near Dalton-in-Furness. This was on very high lying ground and looked out over the estuary towards Millom. The owner, Frank Charles also ran a glider club from here and was a daredevil sort of chap, who was also into speedway riding. Once the tractor and implements were on the farm they were usually left there until the job was finished and my father would travel on his motorcycle every day to work there. They would use an old car to tow the glider to enable it to get into the air. This day the young chap was not driving the car fast enough and Frank Charles turned to my father and said, "Can you show this lad how to go down the hill like bloody hell so that he can get this glider airborne!' The reward being, a glider trip over Barrow and Walney. My father did not need asking twice and the feat was soon accomplished and he was duly rewarded and thoroughly enjoyed his flight! About a year later, father sadly read that Frank Charles had been tragically killed in a glider accident.

My father and uncles were all keen on motorcycling. I remember my father telling me that his first bike he had when he was eighteen was a Montgomery. He also had a Rudge Ulster, that he said was very fast, and a Matchless 500cc. The last bike he owned was a Triumph Speed Twin and he sold that to a man in Ambleside in 1948. Father's brother George was sadly later killed on an International Norton, which was also a very fast bike, at Millthrop, near Sedbergh, in 1938, the year I was born. Uncle George had been both a butcher, as well as farmer. He used to go round the farms in a three-wheeler van delivering meat and sausages. His route took him round, Sedbergh, Dent, Garsdale, Cautley, Middleton and Kirkby Lonsdale. Father's stepbrother, Ernest Armistead also sadly met his fate on a motorbike in 1948–49 whilst he had been working as a farm worker at Pilling in Lancashire.

My father worked for a time as a wagon driver at Jordan's the feed merchants, that was at the top of Allhallows Lane, Kendal, (now houses) and they used to deliver feedstuffs to the local farms.

Dad and mum on his Rudge Ulster at Silverthwaite Quarry, Skelwith Bridge, Ambleside in early 1930s.

Jordan's Granary at the top of Allhallows Lane. *Margaret Duff Collection*

Fred Burns delivering wood at Skelwith Bridge in the mid 1930s.

He later went to work for George Crowsdale, at Haverthwaite, a timber merchant. He was employed there as a tractor driver hauling timber out of the woods, one was from Claiffe Heights, near the old Ferry Inn on Windermere.

In March 1940 when my younger sister, Elizabeth (Libby) was born, I was sent to stay with my Aunt Dorothy and Uncle Fred Burns who lived in the cottage at the Saw Mill they owned at Skelwith Bridge. I was only two at the time. They had two children who were much older than me, Marie and Teddy. During the war they made pit props for use down the coalmines and I remember them being stacked in a shed to dry. All the timber had been brought out of the woods by horses and loaded into the wagons with 'three legs', the name given to a large wooden winch used to lift the large logs onto the awaiting horse and trailer. This was simply made up of three very strong posts that formed a tripod (ends secured in the ground) with a pulley wheel attached near the top of the three posts with a wire rope passing through it. The wire was then attached to the length of wood and was pulled by a horse attached to the other end of the rope. Another horse would have manoeuvred a trailer ready for the heavy length of wood to be lowered onto it. Later with the coming of mechanisation they had a caterpillar tractor they used for snigging timber (hauling) out of the wood. They used Bedford wagons and at the top of the yard there was a big crane and this was worked by hand. It was used to lift tree trunks onto a bogey and then they were carried on the small railway into the sawmill. A large travelling saw bench driven by a Crossley 10 hp open crank engine was used for sawing most of the wood and was wound through by hand. It was started in very cold weather by using a blowlamp on it – how things have progressed for the better. Never mind the good old days!

My Auntie Dorothy wrote to my mother at this time saying, 'Billy has settled down well although he is quite a handful, liking nothing better than going into the yard and watching the men at work!' Later I returned home to find my new baby sister Libby.

When my mother went shopping our next-door neighbour, Mrs Pentith, a music teacher who worked from home, used to look after us. Her husband, Arthur had a butchers shop in Sandes Avenue, Kendal (he was previously manager at the Co-op butchers) and they had two children, Howard and Janet.

We always had a great day out when we went by Ribble Bus (Stagecoach now) to see my mother's brother, Uncle Harry and Auntie Bertha, who had retired due to asthma to Crag Mill Cottages, Skelwith

Bridge. He then went to work at the saw mill at Skelwith Bridge, for his brother-in-law Fred Burns. They had farmed at Millbeck Farm, Langdale until 1936 and had kept Herdwick sheep. He used to tell me about when the sheep sometimes went down onto the rock ledges for the fresh green grass but became crag fast (unable to climb back up). Harry and a friend would go with some rope that they would secure one end round a rock and usually lower Harry down so that he could put the sheep into a sack and be pulled back up to safety. They were not always lucky – sometime the crag fast sheep would jump to its death. Sometimes the mist would come down when Harry was up on the fells and he used to have to wait until it cleared and was safe. In heavy snowfalls sheep could be stuck in snowdrifts for up to three or four weeks before they were found and dug out alive – thanks to his sheep dogs. When Coniston Foxhounds were hunting in the Langdales terriers would be used where foxhounds could not go. They could go down the crevices, then a piece of rope would sometimes be dangled down with a piece of meat on it with the hope that the terrier would latch on and be pulled back up to safety.

We also would visit my mother's sister Auntie Sue (Pepper) and her husband Ernest, who was a joiner and cabinetmaker at Grass Riggs and I would sometimes go to stay. They had no mains water, what water they had came from a well in the cellar that had to be pumped up by hand. When I was small I remember standing on a box to pump the water into the tank but soon became tired.

About once a month we would go to Greenwood Haw, Dent to see my Grandma Armistead and her husband Bob in the Ford Eight car my father had bought in 1937. The earth closet (toilet) was at the bottom of the orchard and you had to be a good runner if you were not to be taken short! This could also prove a difficult job in the dark when you had to take a candle. I have vivid memories of knocking my sister Libby off the wall and into the midden and being smacked!

In 1941 father went to work for the 'War Ag' as a tractor driver based at their Oxenholme Depot. They were organised and run by the Westmorland War Agricultural Committee, in Kendal, that had been set up in 1915 for the previous war and had been reinstated again at the beginning of the Second World War.

The farmers did not have tractors on the farms in those days – they just worked with horses. So when production of food had to be stepped up and Britain had to be made more self-sufficient (enemy submarines attacking food convoys), in order to be able to feed our nation, the men of the War Ag were required to speed up production on the land.

Stable block at Oxenholme House used by War Ag. NFT in later years had this as a depot before it was later knocked down for houses. *Margaret Swanton*

Jobs at the Oxenholme Depot (old stable block at Oxenholme House) were allocated to the men by Parker Hodgson who had to go round the local farms and tell the farmers what land they had to set aside for ploughing and growing of crops. The Board of Agriculture and Fisheries stipulated by law what the farmers had to grow and how much they had to grow. It was laid down that they had to rotate what they grew – oats, corn, turnips, mangels, potatoes and kale for stock feed. There would be about fifty people working from there, including office staff, storeman, foreman, mechanics, agricultural contractors and staff.

My father got his instructions every day where he had to go and what he had to do. His area covered, Burneside, Staveley, Crook, Troutbeck, Windermere, Ambleside and Langdale. His main job was ploughing, with a Fordson tractor and two-furrow plough that was either a Ransome or a Cockshutt. I was only a young boy of eight at the time and I used to love going with my father to the farms, I would sit up on the big wide mud-guard and hang on going over the bumps. Usually after an hour or so I would get bored and go for a walk or do a bit of fishing, before joining my father again. There was also a ploughing and reseeding scheme that began during the war whereby the farmers received grant-aided subsidies and this helped to improve the land greatly.

Dad driving the War Ag green Fordson tractor. Note the metal spade·lugs.

The tractors at that time either had spud wheels or rubber tyres. The spud wheels were steel wheels and these were used for getting a better grip on the steeper ground. In these days there was no four-wheel drive that we have today!

On wet days they used to stay at the Depot and catch up with repairs. They would have their meals in the bate room and if there was nothing to do they would get the playing cards out. The men were paid £5.7s.6d (£5.38) per week.

Here are some of the local men that father new who used to work out of the Oxenholme Depot:

- Tom Smith and Arthur 'Artie' Cheeseman – tractor drivers – both retired and living in Natland.
- Percy Ellwood – tractor driver – binder and threshing – lived on Burneside Road, Kendal (sadly dead).
- Bert Hill – tractor driver – binder – 'jack of all trades' – looked after thresher – sat on binder cutting corn – Bowston Farm, near Kendal (sadly dead).
- Bob Jackson (good friend of fathers) – covered the Lyth Valley area – tractor driver lived over there (sadly dead).
- Bill Shaw – tractor driver – Massey Harris tractor and threshing outfit – from Milnthorpe.
- Bob Atkinson – tractor driver – general work.
- Foreman – Parker Hodgson – he used to go round the farms to organise the work – he had a Hillman Minx with the bottom falling out of it!
- Ken Illingworth – mechanic on the tractors and caterpillar tractors – Sedgwick – sadly dead.
- Bob Wilson – caterpillar tractor driver – D2 – they came over from America.
- Teddy Mason – mechanic and also Mr O'Loughlin, from Kendal.

Father told me about going this day in 1944 to Gowan Bank Farm, Ings, where there were about nine Ukranian prisoners of war, digging drains by hand (spade), while father was ploughing and a guard was looking after them. The prisoners came from Bela Prisoner of War Camp, near Milnthorpe where there were also German and Italians as well. The Germans were really good workers, some came from small farming families and enjoyed the work because they got good meals on the farms. They also helped with the threshing and father became very friendly with one or two of them and would give them cigarettes. Some of the prisoners

War Ag driver on an International TD6 caterpillar tractor with a Massey Harris Prairie Buster Single Furrow Plough (Lease and Lend Scheme) at Greyhound Farm, (just of Paddy Lane) Kendal. *Kathleen Dawson (nee Scott)*

stayed in England after the war and never went back home to their families in the eastern part of Germany because of the harsh regime. This was because after the war Germany was split into East and West Germany and the East was in the hands of the Russians and the West in the hands of the British, French and Americans. The Italians came later and they were very good with their hands and could make cigarette lighters, rings and bracelets out of aluminium – father said they also liked the lassies!

Father and his mates were kept busy most of the year round. In springtime he would be busy ploughing and sowing the corn as seeding by then was done with the corn drill. A man was required to stand on the board at the back to work the lever, working it on and off at the end of rows. These drills were made by Shearer and came from Australia. In the backend they had cutting and threshing. They would start threshing in September and this would continue into early spring. They went round the farms in a threshing gang and would sometimes stay on outlying farms.

Father told me about threshing at Beatrix Potter's farm at Hill Top, at Near Sawrey, Hawkshead, in the 1940s. Tom Story was the farm manager and father used to stop with him if it was very wet. He knew Beatrix

Threshing time at Bridge Stone Farm during the 1940s. Ted Black on top of thresher with Percy Ellwood. Jack Moffat is standing with the horse and James Black (Snr) – wearing a long coat. Second from right is Bert Hill. Centre – is a German prisoner of war standing with the bag of chaff (husks). The Barn has now been converted to a house.

Potter reasonably well and used to see her often walking about in her clogs, hessian sack over her shoulders and an old mackintosh underneath to keep the rain off. She also wore a hessian (coarse) apron around her waist. She had another farm at Troutbeck Park, Windermere.

Tom Smith who lived at Plantation Bridge, covered the same area as father. They took the self-binder to Burneside one evening to be ready for the next day but as it was a moonlight night they decided to stay and cut the field. Another day they were at Staveley, Tom, Dad and Bert Hill. Bert was on the driving wheel of the binder when it hit a rock and he fell off. Fortunately Bert was none the worse.

Bob Ellison had a smallholding with a bit of land behind the War Ag and used to keep stock in some of the outbuildings. He was a bit of a character; smoked black twist and told many a good story. George Lowthian, a railwayman, kept hens near the Depot.

In 1948 when father finished with the War Ag he set up on his own. Little did I know then that this is what I was going to do for the rest of my life and one which I wouldn't have swapped.

Right: Henry Hornyold-Strickland (on a Ford Ferguson tractor), Harry Lancaster (on binder) and Alan Wall (farm worker) at Low Sizergh near Kendal, taken during the Second World War.

Me just starting school – taken in back garden at Scarbrook.

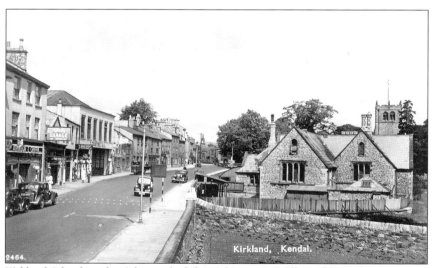

Kirkland School on the right, on the left is Atkinson & Griffin and Z. Crabtree garages. Note the two-way traffic along Kirkland in this 1940s Atkinson and Pollitt picture.
Margaret Duff Collection

II

School Days in Kendal

I STARTED SCHOOL IN 1943 WHEN I WAS FIVE and I went to Kirkland School, Kendal (Kirkland Hall), near the Parish Church. Mother took me to begin with, then I went with Audrey my sister. There were no one-way streets in those days and traffic came both ways over Netherfield Bridge, but the good thing was there was little of it.

My teachers I remember were Miss Haygarth and Mrs Bush. There was no uniform and I just wore a shirt, pullover, brown corduroy shorts, knee length socks, boots or shoes. The teachers had a blackboard and easel and we sat at our desks. I was very shy at first. We used to play all sorts of games out in the playground and some were seasonal like conkers. We also played, marbles, tiggy, whip and top and hopscotch. There were two separate toilet blocks at the bottom of the yard for the girls and boys. We went to the Parish Church for special services and held our sports on the nearby Abbot Hall grounds. I remember my two sisters and I got ringworm and unfortunately I got it quite badly on the head and had most of my hair shaved off. Not very nice!

Some of my schoolmates at that time were Peter Bowden, Gordon Atkinson, Howard Pentith, Brian Fishwick, Alan Prickett and Mildrid Prickett (whose father was an electrician at K' Shoes); Mavis Hesmondhalgh and Josephine Mitchell.

During the war years we had quite a lot of evacuees attending our school from Manchester and Liverpool and some had obviously come from fairly rough areas and fights were not uncommon. When out on the playground one day I remember seeing fifteen Bren Gun carriers going over Netherfield Bridge heading south, this caused quite a stir! We also used to see Pickfords low-loaders carrying ships' boilers en-route to Barrow shipyards and large Royal Air Force Bedford wagons carrying aircraft parts.

As part of the war effort we collected rosehips (3d [2p] per lb) and took them to school where they were weighed and collected and sent away to make rosehip syrup. We also collected copper and aluminium

The canal at Parkside Road, Kendal with gas works in the distance. I used to often make my way home from school along the towpath. *Margaret Duff Collection*

Dilly Bridge on the outskirts of Natland Road in May 1975 before it was demolished, the hardcore for the new road underneath. Old road to right (just before Watercrook on way into Kendal). *Margaret Swanton*

pans that were to be used for the war effort. In my keenness to help I went with the older lads who had an old pram to put the scrap in. Iron railings were also removed from outside buildings and workmen used oxyacetylene torches. The blackout was part of life for us and my mother was forever saying, 'Keep those curtains closed!' The nearest bomb that was dropped was at Cooper House Farm, Selside in April 1941 where eleven were killed and two injured; there was another at Grange when a bomber lightened his load. After school my mother would sometimes take us for a walk up Peter's Lane (pathway midway up Oxenholme Road that cuts through to Kendal Parks and Sedbergh Road) to collect water-cress. Father was in the Home Guard and their meetings were held at Hawesmead House, (now gone), Kendal.

The Kendal to Lancaster canal was at the back of our house and we used to fish there in the summer months catching perch, pike and eels. When we fished for pike (an ugly fish) we used to put a small perch on our hook as bait and when we caught one and tried to take it of the hook they could sometimes give you a nasty nip if you were not careful. During the winter months we would go sledging on the Mayday Field (now part of K' Shoes) and in 1947 when it was a particularly hard winter we were able to skate on the canal with Gordon and Malcolm Gorst; Edward and Robin Petty; and Peter Bowden, and we skated all the way from Highgate

My sisters Audrey and Libby taken in 1949 in the Mayday Field.

Settlings (above Leisure Centre) as far as Cracalt Bridge, near Kendal. Workmen used a works barge when they were repairing leaks and keeping the towpath clear, when it was moored up at weekends we used to sometimes take it up the canal for a ride and sometimes got it stuck. The last barge came up from Preston with coal in 1944. The canal was drained about 1950 and in 1960 it was filled in with rubbish from Kendal to Natland. The canal had closed because competition between the railways and road haulage eventually made it uneconomic. There were four bridges on that stretch of canal (from our house on Natland Road) Natland Mill Beck; Dilly Bridge; Natland Hall and Crow Park. Dilly Bridge was taken down in 1975 when the road was altered just beyond the K Shoe factory at Watercrook. It was named after William Dilworth Crewdson of Helme Lodge who had his own landing stage there. Today plans are going ahead for the re-opening of the canal after years of work and planning and hopefully in the very near future we will be able to see canal boats once more travelling up through from Preston into Kendal.

One of the jobs I did at home for mum was collecting firewood, chopping the kindling and bringing in coal for the fire. Gallowbarrow, which was just a couple of hundred yards from us on Natland Road, was the Corporation Tip at this time (now a small housing estate). Years ago it was the town's gallows, though there is no record of anyone ever being hanged there. We used to have great fun rummaging for old bicycle parts to build bikes and jordies (bogies) with. Sand Martins used to build their nests in the sandbank there. Howies the builders who had a business just off South Road prior to it being the tip used to remove sand from there.

Peddlers used to come round in those days selling their wares, mother told me about one that used to come round sharpening scissors and knifes, and he carried his tool bag on his back. He slept rough and mum would give him tea and maybe make him a cheese sandwich. He used to come up on the coal barges in the 1930s and worked on the farms doing seasonal jobs when extra staff was required for thinning turnips and at hay and harvest time.

I used to enjoy building forts down by the river and these were built of sods and stones, with sheets of tin for the roof. Inside if we were lucky, an old piece of carpet was put on the floor and a sack was hung over the doorway – we pretended we were Ancient Britons!

We would also make rafts using oil drums as floats, these we would find on K Shoes dump (empty solution drums and scraps of shoe leather) and boards on top to sit on. They didn't always float but when they did, we would paddle across to Scroggs, at Watercrook, where it was imperative we stopped before disappearing over the weir. The part of the riverbank we were trying to get to had been washed away and a small cave had formed and we would tie a rope to a nearby tree and abseil down, as it was very steep. We would then make a fire and bake potatoes – it was great! We sometimes saw otters, I remember seeing one at Hawes Bridge. It was all good clean fun.

Looking through my mother's diary on 9 June 1944 she has written that 'A policeman called to say that Billy was found pushing a hencoop into the river!' That was the time that Peter Bowden and me pushed Thomas Metcalfe's coop into the river – it is believed it had fighting cocks in it. I got a good whacking for it and father had to make a new coop. I don't know what happened to the birds – there was only probably a couple in it and they flew out.

Also when the river was low at Watercrook Farm we used to cross the weir (this powered the waterwheel for the Gawith and Hoggarth Snuff Mill at Helsington Laithes) and play with the Chaplow boys who had an old BSA motorbike. So as you can imagine we had a good time. The Chaplows were well known threshing contractors and had large traction engines that used to pull the threshers to the various local farms they travelled to. They also had steamrollers and during the summer months Westmorland County Council hired them for road maintenance, for rolling in the chippings during tar spraying. Their tarmacing business is still going strong today.

Nat Bell farmed at Watercrook Farm and his three sons Ronald, Philip and John, went to Kirkland School with us. Nat grew oats, turnips, carrots and peas. We were bits of rascals and would crawl up the rows picking peas and carrots. Sometimes Nat would see us and run after us but needless to say we were faster on our feet and he never caught us!

In December 1944, Libby was taken ill with scarlet fever and was taken by ambulance to the Isolation Hospital this was in the zinc building set behind Change Bridge, just off Lound Street. I can remember going to see her and only being allowed to wave to her through the window. She was only four and when she got better she was allowed home to convalesce and gradually got better.

Saturday afternoons there was always a matinee to look forward to at the Palladium on Sandes Avenue and we used to catch the Dallam Bus (country bus service from Milnthorpe, forerunner to Ribble, now Stagecoach). The fare was 2d (1p) and 6d (3p) into the pictures. Hop-a-long Cassidy (a cowboy), Tarzan and Laurel and Hardy were some of my favourites – though it all looks fairly tame and unexciting to what children watch now. I remember Mr Bill Buckley was the commissionaire and he used to work during the week for Kendal Corporation on the coal wagon. The coal depot was on the sidings in the Railway Station Goods Yard. If we were at the Roxy and there was a western on we usually heard George the commissionaire chip in and say, 'Don't get too near the front lads, you will get sand in your eyes!'

When I was ten my mother developed cancer and had a long spell in Christies Hospital Manchester and I went to stay with Issac and Anne Whitwell and their two children, John and Margaret, who lived at Low Longmire Farm, Troutbeck. They looked after me as if I was one of their own and I remember them taking me out on trips up the Lakes and on the steamers. One of my favourite jobs there was collecting the eggs. I would go with my bucket, which had some straw on the bottom and collect maybe ten eggs. That seemed like a lot but I soon discovered the hens' were laying away and found their secret nests and the bucket would soon fill!

Pig killing day was a big event. The pig's throat was cut and while the pig was being bled, I had to stir the blood to stop it from clotting and this was then mixed with fat, barley and seasoning to make black pudding. It was then put in a large baking tin to set and then cut into slices when required. Boiling water was poured over the pig's skin and its hair

A break during harvesting at Low Longmire Farm in 1946.
Left to right: Issac Whitwell; Bert Hill; John Harrison (Knotts Farm, Troutbeck Bridge);
Mrs Kate Whitwell; Dad - Jack Moffat (on draw bar); John Whitwell; Mary Harrison
and Mr Harrison Snr.

was then scraped off. The various joints would be cut up, covered in salt
(bacon) and saltpetre (round the bones) to preserve, bound together and
tied in rolls with string, then hung from hooks in the kitchen to mature.
The pig's ears and trotters were also used – nothing was wasted. You
would often see black pudding on the farmers' stalls in Kendal market
when they used to come with their produce on a Saturday morning and
sat behind their trestle tables laden with home produce. You got the usual
eggs (hen and duck), homemade produce – butter etc, vegetables and
fruit in season e.g. damsons from the Lyth Valley; lilac and daffodils and
extra festive food and poultry (geese, turkey, chicken, duck and pheas-
ant) at Christmas. They also had stalls down Stramongate and they were
always very popular.

I remember one day when I was feeding the carthorse in the stable. I
had gone into the loft above and shoved some hay down into the rack. I
then went back down to feed it some cake and it stood on my foot, fortunately I was wearing clogs at the time but I still let out a loud scream. My
foot was only bruised but needless to say I was more careful next time.

Tommy Thistlethwaite was a lengths-man employed by Manchester
Corporation Water Works checking the valve houses for leaks in the

water pipe that runs from Thirlmere to Manchester (1881). Tommy's length was from Troutbeck to High Borrans. The valve houses would be sited for easy access in fields and have a protective metal cover over the entrance, which was locked. Once unlocked, he would descend a ladder to the actual water pipe. Tommy would often call at the farm for a brew in the morning and I would sometimes go with him to walk his length. My father and Tommy used to play tricks on each other, one instance I remember was when Tommy once put a dead rabbit under the back seat of our Ford Eight car. There was rather a nasty smell before we found out what it was! Tommy always helped during hay and harvest time and I think it was pretty much his second home as he was so often there. He later moved to Garnett Bridge and later retired.

Another day I was helping to muck out the cows and had to wheel a full barrow of muck (dung) up a plank that was used to get it to the top of the midden – pretty solid state! This day I did not get enough speed up and over the barrow and me went into the muck! Needless to say I was not very popular in more ways than one!

I also went to help cutting the bracken on Moor Howe. Issac and John used scythes and I used a little grass hook (wooden handle with curved metal hook). This was cut when the bracken was brown, stored in a building and later was used for bedding the animals and keeping them warm and clean when inside during the winter months. Tea was taken with us in a basket and we had bread, jam and cheese sandwiches, with gingerbread or apple pasty. This was before thermos flasks came into being and the tea was put in a bottle then slipped inside a thick woollen sock to keep warm. It did the trick!

John and I used to go rabbiting with his ferret, net and snares. We would look for the rabbit holes, cover some with nets and put the ferret down, and it would flush the rabbits out and we would maybe catch two or three at a time. We would pull their necks and slit a cut above their ankle joint and slip the other leg through for ease of carrying. Then we would slide them onto a length of wood and sling it over our shoulder. Sometimes we would catch quite a lot of rabbits and would keep some for the pot and the rest given away to friends and neighbours. You could also sell them for so much each. I also used to go with him when he went shooting carrion crows with his 12 bore shotgun – they were treated as vermin as they used to peck the eyes out of young lambs during lambing time.

Left: The farmers' wife's selling their produce in Stramongate, Kendal, on an autumn Saturday morning in the 1930s. *Margaret Duff Collection*

John was good at woodwork and he made a lot of the farm gates, hurdles, posts and rails. His saw bench had an open crank Rushton and Hornby 8 hp engine which lay for years in the back of his shed, until a few years ago he gave me the engine and I have now restored it.

Mother eventually came home from hospital and had a period of convalescing. The cancer was in remission and she gradually got back into family life but it was a slow process.

Oxenholme Railway Station was a very busy place in the 1950s. Near the sheds the steam engines were turned on a turntable and the drivers would sometimes ask us lads to give them a turn. This we did in the hope of getting a ride on one of the banking engines (on the footplate no less if we were lucky) that assisted fully laden trains up Shap summit. One of the bankers was called 'Kendal Tommy'. If we knew which particular signalman was on duty at Helmside, we would go there for a warm on a cold winter's night.

Oxenholme in those days was a very important railway village and they were well provided for even to the extent of having a reading room (junction of Helmside and Burton Road that is now a house) to relax in and we went there and played billiards, snooker and table tennis. Just opposite on the A65 is the old Mission Hall and this after a time was used as a hardware store and garage for William (Billy) Barnes. He went round the farms in a Commer van selling his hardware eg brushes, tools, Tilley and paraffin lamps and of course paraffin. Peter Kirk, a friend, sometimes worked for him and we would go with him on his rounds, to Howgill, Firbank, Grayrigg, Selside and Patton. Sometimes we would not get back until ten o'clock at night, as Billy was an excellent salesman and could talk people round to buy almost anything. We used to say, 'He could sell sand to the Arabs!' Billy was a real character!

In the late 1940s and early 1950s Kendal Corporation owned Wattsfield Farm and my father used to do most of the tractor work, ploughing, ridging, setting the potatoes and grass cutting for hay. John Nelson, the farmer who rented it, did not live in the farmhouse, this was occupied by Walter Thompson who had a butcher's shop in Highgate Bank, Kendal, his brother-in-law was Milley Robinson, who had the timber merchant's near the hospital. One wet day I was at the farm with my father and John asked me if I wanted a pipe of backie as he smoked black twist. I foolishly said, 'Yes.' I watched eagerly as he filled the pipe for me and got it going. Shortly after taking the first puff I felt both dizzy and sick. An experience I did not wish to repeat in a hurry!

John Airey, another of my dad's friends lived on Natland Road and worked at Crabtrees Garage in Kirkland (now DSG). Later he set up his own garage in Windermere (just beyond Windermere Hotel on the left) selling DMW motorcycles. Both dad and him were motorbike men and they rented part of a building at the farm and in the back of this building Kendal Corporation kept some of their old horse drawn hearses and black coaches. I would sometimes go and sit in the coaches. I didn't stop long as I must admit it always felt a bit eerie in the dark.

The nearest local garage was Vitrix (now Lound Road Garage, next to Kirkbie Kendal School) owned by Billy Dickinson and Mrs Frearson (his daughter) used to work the hand pumps and wore a brown smock. Oil was sold in bottles then.

Bewshers general store was on the Lound, near Netherfield Bridge, and was where we bought our sweets (liquorice, aniseed balls and barley sugar) on the way to school. Arthur Holmes used to have the general store on Rinkfield.

Fred Wilson used to come round with fruit and vegetables on a horse and flat cart. His nickname was 'Baggy Wilson' as he always wore knee breeches and leggings. Johnny Barber also came round in his Austin butcher's van and mother would get all her meat from him. In the 1960s he had a farm at Middle Barrows Green. The Bensons from Flookburgh used to come round with fresh fish and was very popular.

I moved up to secondary school when I was eleven and went to Stramongate when Mr Brockbank was headmaster. We took the usual subjects, English, arithmetic, geography, history, woodwork, metalwork and sports. I remember most had nicknames though I don't know if they actually knew them. Mr Scargill (Punch) took woodwork; Mr Jones (Spike), maths; Mr Hewitt, art and geography; Mr Johnston (Steamboat) metalwork; Joe Lawson took art and science and was synonymous for giving the cane; Bruce Reid took sport; Mr Turner (Sticky Lips) English; Mr Endicote (Pew) practical drawing.

We played cricket and football at school. Sports Day we had the usual, flat race, long jump, high jump and fell race that involved running up to the castle and back. My favourite lessons were English, geography, metalwork and woodwork. I remember Mr Brockbank had a big Rover 90 car. School dinners were good and my favourite was mince and potatoes, which we had accompanied with raw grated carrot or cabbage, and boiled beetroot (no vinegar) followed by apple crumble and custard.

Mr Johnston took metal work, that I really enjoyed and remembered what he said about safety 'that you should always carry tools down by

The inside of the old swimming baths in Allhallows Lane, Kendal in the early 1900s. Just as they were in my day – nothing altered! *Margaret Duff Collection*

your side.' Some of the lads would get into trouble for fighting and such like and were rewarded with 'ten of the best!' We also went swimming to the public baths in Allhallows Lane. It closed on the 19 April 1982 and was until recently Shearman House (South Lakeland District Council offices) – this is now being redeveloped. All that is left is the original name above the main door – Corporation Swimming Bath Laundry and Private Baths! The Leisure Centre in Burton Road, Kendal was opened on 28 April 1982 by the Duke of Gloucester and has a swimming pool and sports facilities.

When I was about twelve I joined the Air Cadets, Mr Plint was in charge of us and we met in the building next to Vitrix Garage. We felt quite smart when marching in parades round town in our uniforms – Air Force blue shirt, trousers, jacket and beret. We did aircraft recognition and I remember as a treat we went to an airfield near York and we all had a flight in an old troop carrier. There were a lot of wartime planes parked up at York and Silloth airfields – Lancaster, Hurricanes and Spitfires.

I was also a member of the YMCA Club and we played snooker or table tennis and in summer went to Lakeside Camp, near Newby Bridge where we did archery, canoeing, building fires, erecting tents and such-like. All good fun!

An electric van ran back and forwards from the K' Shoes Factory at Low Mills to the top factory on Lound Road (now K Shoes Factory shop) carrying goods and for devilment we would jump on the back to get a lift, if the driver saw us in his mirror we would be chased. We nicknamed him 'Enoch!'

Mr and Mrs Crabtree (Crabtree's Garage) lived in a large house called Summer Lodge (where Levens Close is now) and I remember apple scrumping (orchard warbling), they also had a tennis court.

We used to have a few pounds in our pockets now from money we had earned from helping dad and had progressed from pushbikes and were always now on the look out for motorbikes. We would go down to Andy Murphy's Scrap Yard which was down the back of the YMCA. We would say, 'Any good motorbikes in Andy?' He would reply, 'Yes, there is just one come in, she is a real goer boys!' We would get our bikes (BSA, Matchless, Royal Enfield and Ariel) and push them through the town, along waterside, onto Rinkfield then sometimes down the canal to Natland and back. Probably paid thirty shillings or a couple of pounds. We also used to take them on Helm scrambling. Dad would help us to get them going and I learned a lot helping him. The Helm is the fell just off the A65 between Natland and Oxenholme and has panoramic views of the Lakeland Fells, Howgills round to Morecambe Bay, with an Ordnance Survey Trig point on top, and is very popular with walkers.

I was beginning by this time to do quite a lot of work for dad after school and at weekends, even skipping school for bigger jobs as I got older and became more use.

In the 1950s most of the traffic on the roads was wagons and they used to park up at night on New Road car park, next to the River Kent. The drivers would get booked in and spend the night in one of the local boarding houses. The regular drivers would have set digs. I remember some used to have them in two shifts. When one got out of bed another would be ready to climb in, the bed would still be warm! Alexander's fish wagons

This early 1930s picture of snow on the top of Shap and shows what conditions could be like then. *Margaret Duff Collection*

used to travel daily from Aberdeen down to Liverpool and Manchester and changed over drivers on New Road, leaving a fishy smell behind. You must remember of course that there were no heaters in the wagons then and the drivers would have been 'frozen to the bone' if they had tried to sleep in them overnight! On our way to school on frosty mornings it was a common sight to see wagon drivers going through the rigmaroles of trying to get them started up. The night before, the drivers would have drained the water out of the radiators and would fill them up from the Kent the following morning. We were still in the days of no anti-freeze or heaters fitted to start the engine. There weren't many self-starters whereby you just had to press a button, the driver still had to turn the engine on the old starting handle by putting the engine into full compression, a rope was then wound round the handle and he would pull it over. Sometimes if he saw us he would maybe say, 'Give us a hand lads,' and we would only be too happy to lend a hand. It usually took three people to pull them over and could take up to half-an-hour to get one wagon started.

In wintertime Shap on the A6 was notorious for being closed by snow and the drivers would sometimes stay the night in the Parish Hall if all the digs were full. Snowploughs and blowers would try to keep Shap open but they were not always successful as there was no salt in those days until the late 1950s, prior to this limestone dust and fine chippings were used. Some would maybe get as far as the Jungle Café (now Kendal Caravans) Selside, a very well known transport café in those days, open 24 hrs, they could be stranded there for two or three days at a time. Well-known 'ladies of the road' were reputed to tout their trade there!

Also on the lay-by at the top of Shap there was another café for drivers, this was made up of two buses being permanently parked up back to back. Shap in those days was very busy being on the main A6 road north to south route (no M6 motorway until 1971) and wagons of course were not as powerful then and had the long hard drag sometimes nose to tail up the summit, with many breakdowns and mishaps.

Right: Another wintry scene on Shap in the 1970s. Conditions don't look quite as bad! Shown on the left is an AEC, Leyland Super Comet and ERF wagons.
Margaret Duff Collection

Telephone: KENDAL 1408

J. W. MOFFAT

Agricultural Contractor

★ PICK-UP BALING

★ THRESHING

★ PLOUGHING

★ LIME SPREADING

NATLAND   KENDAL

Advertisement in the 1959 NFU Telephone Directory.

Spring cleaning the thresher at Ashfield in 1958. Dad, Colin Wharton on the ladder and me at the bottom.

III

Agricultural Contractor

FATHER STARTED WORKING FOR HIMSELF as an agricultural contractor in 1949 after he had finished working for the War Ag and would no doubt have had a good list of customers to be able to set out on his own. So with the money he had saved and had left to him, he used this to buy the machinery he needed to start and proudly bought his first tractor, a Standard Fordson, made at Dagenham. He also bought a brand new Tullis threshing machine from Rickerby's at Penrith (salesman then was Mr Box) and this had been built in Aberdeen costing £900 – which was a lot of money then. Rickerby's had put it on display on their stand at the Westmorland Agricultural Show, at the Showfield on Shap Road (Morrison's etc now on) in Kendal. Dad also acquired an International two-furrow plough, a cultivator, ridging plough, a Bamford mowing machine and Albion self-binder. Dad acquired some of the machinery from the War Ag, agricultural engineers and various sales. He bought a converted horse self-binder from Colonel Crewdson at Helm Lodge who had Natland Millbeck Farm then. Also bought from Tom Hoggarth's on Sandes Avenue.

As well as looking after us, mother now took on the responsible job of doing dad's books (paperwork). Dad had good grounding in this as he had seen how the War Ag billed farmers when they had done work, so he had a good idea of what records required keeping. So dad kept a diary and recorded everything in it, what he was doing that particular day, where he was at, how many hours or acres he did, who was there and machinery used. These details proved invaluable later when mother sent out the bills. Dad advertised in the NFU Directory and Kendal Auction but mainly got his work via word of mouth. He would also apply for various local contracts so that he was kept busy all the year round, to the extent that he eventually had to take on workers, both full and part-time, plus of course more machinery. He took Jimmy Cross from Staveley on full time and part-time Derek Harbey, who lived in Rinkfield, Kendal.

The first lot of Standard Ferguson tractors that came from Banner Lane Coventry to Kendal after the Second World War. *Margaret Duff Collection*

When people wanted jobs doing, they either phoned or popped round to see us. He either charged per hour or per acre or for the complete job depending on what it was and the type of land. Usually we were paid when the job was finished, sent them a bill or took it round, dependant on who it was. Some were bad payers and didn't pay you until the following year when they wanted the job doing again, or if it was a small bill the farmer would maybe say, 'would you like a few eggs, a piece of home cured bacon or maybe a bag of potatoes.'

His work was all seasonal, dependant on the weather, fitting other jobs in as you went along, as well as on wet days doing any repairs. Often it could be pretty much continual work for long spells at a time and social and family life had to be fitted in as best it could. Many of the time there was never enough hours in the day – but when the work was there you just kept on going.

I used to help dad quite a lot as I had learned to drive the tractor. Before this I used to sit on the tractor with my father when he went ploughing with the Standard Fordson. I would sit in front of the gear lever, it was quite warm with the heat from the back axle. I used to watch my father closely changing gears and when he was ploughing he used to say, 'Do you want to have a go?' I was only 8 or 9 years old at the time when he was working for the War Ag. I would steer it a bit to start with. Then when I got a bit older dad gave me the chance to drive, he got it going in first gear then we would change seats and I would take over and eventually learn to change gear into 2nd and 3rd. Only one lever, once for clutch and press down again for the brake. I really enjoyed it. Did little jobs like disc harrowing and I used to drive a little Ferguson when I was 12 years old that dad bought. It was easier to drive and manoeuvre.

Early tractors only went at 4 mph and you could get different gearing whereby the tractor went quicker, up to 10 mph, known as high top gear. They started on petrol and when they got warmed up in about five minutes they were turned over, by turning a small brass tap under the fuel tank onto TVO In very cold weather you would put a hessian sack over the front of the radiator so it would warm up quickly. This was called a blind and some tractors were fitted with it and this was pulled up from the bottom of the radiator. Later dad bought an International W6, a far better tractor. They came over from America under the Lease and Lend Scheme during the war and we got ours in 1944–45. This was far more powerful. These tractors went on to the mid 50s, then about 1952–53 the diesels came in, these were more efficient and economical, importantly they were fitted with the hydraulic lift and this did away with trailing

Derek Harbey and dad in Kendal. The International W6 tractor (Lease and Lend) on the left and Ford Ferguson on the right..

machinery, like ploughing and mowing machines (all had wheels on). This obviously made it a lot easier carrying implements.

Dad's year would start in the spring with ploughing, sowing corn, oats and barley, preparing the ground for turnips. In April the ground had to be ridged up for potatoes and kale and mangels to be drilled (sown).

Hay time would start in June and would go on to the end of July. When dad was mowing locally around Natland, he would go with the Fergy and mowing machine and set it up in the field for me. Then I would go down on my old black Raleigh bike after school and cut till I was finished or till it got dark and came home sometimes at ten at night on my bike.

I sometimes also skipped school if they were very busy and sometimes got the job of driving the tractor and hay sweep. The hay sweep was attached to the front of the tractor and some even lifted up and down, if connected to hydraulics. It would be about six to seven feet wide and the pitch pine poles had metal tips. The hay was swept to the stationary baler (no pick-up balers then) and the bales were tied by hand.

Then harvest-time was from the end of August through to September, cutting corn with the self-binder and my job was riding on the binder working the levers. I remember eight months after getting our thresher, Jimmy had taken it home to Natland Road this day to park it up but ended up accidentally throwing it over on its side and blocked the road. Pennington's had to come with a large crane to right it.

Then from September to March we had threshing, sawing wood and muck spreading. We took on other jobs as the years went on like hedging and contract work – including lime spreading, reseeding after pipe laying, snow ploughing for the Council and cutting canal sidings.

Dad covered pretty much the same area as he had done in the War Ag and gradually this area increased as he took on more and more work.

Another of our customers was Jeff Swift who in 1951 came to Dry Howe Farm, Selside, which was a big sheep farm. Dad and I did a lot of work for Jeff. We spread all his muck, made a lot of bridges to cross all the streams that run through the fields. A lot of larch trees were felled and Jeff brought them down by horse one at a time from Horse Shoe Wood. With our tractor and saw bench we managed to make a lot of fencing posts, rails and a piles of firewood. Later we did muck spreading, grass mowing and pick-up baling for him. He was a good customer.

IV

Threshing

WHEN I WAS NOT AT SCHOOL (which as you have read was quite often dependant on the season and weather at the time) I used to go with dad and the threshing outfit to local farms, this was usually from late September to March. Threshing or as I call it thrashing, is the separating of the seed grain from the husks (chaff) and straw. When we first started threshing we would work an area out like Natland, Sedgwick, Hincaster and Milnthorpe. Then we would move on to another area like Grayrigg, Whinfell and Selside then on to Tebay, Orton, Greenholme, Raisbeck, Sunbiggin and Gaisgill. Work was usually pre-booked from the year before and you would begin on the lowland farms and end with hill farms. Each farmer would help each other in that particular area by sending somebody on threshing day and you could maybe have had up to sixteen people to lend a hand and get the job done as quickly as possible.

Getting the thresher to the farm was a job in itself and my job was brakeman on steep hills. We would leave home early (7.30-8.30 am) to set the thresher and baler up. We couldn't start too early as the farmers had to have time to complete the milking and other early morning jobs. We had the onerous task of getting the slow moving cumbersome machinery weighing some eight tons there and then negotiating the awkward narrow farm gateways, that all took time and effort. A brakeman was essential when travelling on particularly bad roads such as the one (A685) out to Tebay. First we had to contend with Spital Brow. To enable us to go up, we had to hook off the baler and take the thresher up first, then come back for the baler and then carried on to the next steep hill at Hayfell and repeat the procedure. Next and perhaps the worst was Docker Brow as it also had a bad bend in it, then down Grayrigg Hawes to Low Borrow Bridge, after that it was good going! You must remember we had it all to do again when coming home but in reverse order!

Left: Harry Lancaster (Snr) thatching and his sons Harry (Jnr) on the left and Jimmy standing below at Low Sizergh Farm around 1940. *J. H. Cookson, Kendal/Jimmy Lancaster*

Threshing at Natland Hall in 1960.
Left to right: Dad talking to Jack Procter at the 'donkey's head'. Bobby Dodgson wearing a hat, on top of thresher and Tony Wilson forking sheaves from trailer.

Close up view of the same scene showing Johnny Dodgson (Snr) standing beside the tractor, Tony Wilson on the trailer and Bobby Dodgson on top of thresher.

When we arrived we had to set up (if a big job we would maybe do it the night before) and a long belt would run from the tractor to the thresher and another from the thresher to the baler – remembering at the same time that the thresher and baler had to be level. The corn sheaves requiring to be threshed would either be stored in stacks (ricks) in the yard (stack yard) near the farm or in a stone building. They would either be conical shaped (very few round our way), where they were thatched near the top and the point covered with hessian. Most common round here were the large oblong stacks, slightly raised in the middle and covered by a large canvas sheet, weighed down round the sides by lengths of wood or stone to keep the rain (weather) out. We used to thresh the stacks first as they were more vulnerable to the weather and then from inside in bad weather. Some farmers wanted the stationary baler with the big heavy bales and we also had what we called the press for lightweight bales. The corn was put into hessian bags and these were carted away by tractor and trailer, or carried on their backs and tipped loose onto the granary floor. Feeding stuff (cake for the cattle) was supplied from the provender (feed) merchant in hessian bags and the farmers kept them (from previous years) and this was one of the uses they were put to. The chaff (waste and husks) was usually put into the bales to get rid of it or put into a shed in bags (one of my jobs) and used to mix in with feed turnips and such like. Threshing started about November and would go on to about the middle of March. The straw was sometimes chopped and used for mixing in with the feed or just used for bedding to keep the animals warm that were kept inside during the winter.

It was certainly a big day in the farming calendar. The farmer's wife provided the meals and dinner would maybe be a tatty hash followed by rice pudding and tea to wash it down. You must remember in those days, the same plate would probably be used for both courses – you had to make sure you wiped up the gravy before you got your rice pudding – though sometimes the tell tale gravy line round the side was still visible!

One day while thrashing just outside Kendal, at Mr Lund's at Benson Hall, they caught one hundred and thirty-five rats! This was quite common (not the amount), when the stacks were being threshed, for the rats to be sheltering in the bottom of the last stack under the stones or the boarding that had been put down to keep the sheaves off the ground. Sometimes a fence would be erected around the outside and the farm dogs or terriers put in. The rest of the farmers etc would be standing round with pitchforks and as the last sheaves were thrown out the rats that were hiding would run out and make a bid to escape. They would try and run up the posts, through or under the fence – they could be fearsome, trying to bite the dog – anything in a bid to escape with their lives. Farmers used to tell tales of mice or rats running up their legs and it was not uncommon if they were not wearing gaiters for them to tie string round their trousers bottoms or just below the knee. Would you want a mouse or rat running up your leg?

We charged so much an hour for the threshing and extra for the baler. There was a separate charge setting up of the machinery – in the 1950s it was £1.10s.0d. (£1.50). Then on top of that it was £1.10s.0d. an hour for me and my father. It all mounted up but it was still reasonable and we always did a good job. Dad was a hard worker and everybody had to work accordingly.

Note: In 1963 combine harvesters replaced the threshing machine, it was a lot faster and did not need as many men to work it.

V

Hay Time

I N THE 1950S THE GRASS WAS CUT IN JUNE for hay with a Ferguson cutter bar mower and the baling was done with a Ross stationary baler (made in Wales) that was driven by a long belt from the tractor. Having no knotters on to tie the string this had to be done by hand. We always carried three spare knives in a special case or sheaf. The knives reciprocated. We always had to sharpen them every night in preparation for the next day.

The hay was swept to the baler, by a tractor and hay sweep and forked in by hand. Sometimes the bales were carted away with a tractor and trailer and sometimes they were stacked in the field and sheeted up. This job was done on an hourly rate.

In 1952 we got our first pick-up baler this was an International B45 and came from Norman Croft's, in Wildman Street. Hay time was made much easier with the new baler. Bales were charged at 6d (3p) each. The drawback of this baler was that we had to widen the gates, as it was seven feet wide. A radius of about ten miles was covered and the days were very long; mowing in the early morning then breaking off about eleven o'clock and starting baling sometimes till midnight, seven days a week, weather permitting and ending with the hill farms up Orton and Tebay.

When hay timing the farmer's wife would come into the field with a basket full of sandwiches – beef, cheese etc, cakes and apple pasties and sometimes followed by strawberries and cream. The tea came in a can and sometimes in a bottle. It was always warmly welcomed and time for a short break before commencing again.

A big day's baling was 3,000 bales. Later we got a New Holland 68 baler that was also from Croft's. Drum mowers came out in the early 1960s and these were a lot faster than the cutter bars and you could cut about five acres an hour. Extra fuel had to be carried with us in drums as we were working long hours and we could use an awful lot of fuel. A special rack was also fitted on the back of the tractor to carry the baler twine – later this was red or blue plastic string.

Hay scene at Dodgson's, Natland Hall in early 1950s. Bob Bindloss is on the tractor sweeping hay. John Chapman is forking hay and father is on the right.

Father tying the string on the bales manually as was the norm. Alf Bennett forking hay.

Father on the right. Note the labouring saving device of using a ladder in pre-elevator days. The momentum of the bales coming out of the baler shoves the earlier bales along.

Me driving one of the new International B45 pick-up balers at Natland Hall in 1959.

Our bungalow 'Ashfield' Hawes Lane, Natland in 1956.

Our yard with two Fordson Major tractors parked and a corn drill on the trailer in 1961–62.

VI

Moving to Natland and starting work with Dad

I N 1953 WE MOVED TO THE VILLAGE OF NATLAND, just over a mile from where we lived on Natland Road on the outskirts of Kendal. We acquired quarter of an acre of land from Anthony John Armistead in 1952, who owned at that time Natland Hall and our parcel of land was just a few hundred yards down Hawes Lane on the right. We had outgrown Natland Road and we needed buildings to accommodate our machinery. There was a large ash tree on our plot so we aptly called it 'Ashfield' and built a three bed-roomed bungalow and large shed to house our growing business.

The foundations we dug ourselves with the help of school friend Peter Bowden. We employed local builders Charnley, Purvis and Newby to build it. A good neighbour of ours for many years, Pearson Charnley, was the painter and decorator, his family were living at Park Close; Donald Purvis the joiner lived at Sedgwick; and John Newby the builder came from Kendal. Ours was the first bungalow built on the lane. My mother's one stipulation was that there should be a very large walk-in airing cupboard to dry all our frequently wet clothes, as there were no cabs on the tractors in those days. All the girders for the shed came from the slate quarries at the top of Longsledale and the sheets of corrugated sheeting came from the old Shorts Factory (sea planes) at White Cross Bay, Troutbeck Bridge, near Windermere. The bungalow and building came to £3,200. As you can see dad kept a note of everything in his diaries and those have proved invaluable in writing this book.

Natland of course in those days was quite small; as we obviously did not have all the new houses we have today. The green was split with roads criss-crossing through the middle of it. Park Close was built in 1947 to house farm workers. We had the village school, Church, village hall, Post Office, blacksmiths, smithy buildings (actual farm buildings owned by the Moorhouse family – now houses) – Arthur Brown had a joiners shop

Park Close, Natland at the time of road widening in 1960.

there (later his son Alan became the joiner) and was also a builder. Jack Howson had Smithy buildings before this.

My family all moved into the bungalow in March 1953 without me as I was in Westmorland County Hospital, Kendal with rheumatic fever. This had started when I was at Stramongate School and my condition deteriorated and in the February of that year I was taken by ambulance from 'Scarbrook' Natland Road and admitted to hospital (East View – now Summerhill old peoples home). With rheumatic fever the main conditions are fever and arthritis of many joints; it can affect the heart whereby you have a rapid pulse, chest pain and breathlessness. In those days it was very serious and people died of it. I was in the male medical ward, with ten beds down each side. I had to lie flat on my back for six weeks so that I put no strain on the heart and had to use bed bottles and bedpans. I had penicillin injections every four hours. Some of the nurses that looked after me on the ward were Lena Willan, Ruth Ibbotson, Jean Trevaskis (Polish) were extra kind to me, perhaps because I was the youngest? Sister Price was very strict but matron was boss. I was fed strained soup from a drinking cup to begin with but as I recovered I was able to enjoy my meals sitting up and was able to go to the toilet in a wheelchair. When it was warm I was wheeled out onto the balcony. I remember Sister Price on a night would come round asking what you would like to drink and in one deep breath would say, 'Hot milk, cold milk, Ovaltine, Horlicks or what, how much bread and butter?' I was in for three months and came

1960s photo showing the Post Office, Natland on the right.

out in May looking like 'a beanpole' to our new bungalow in Natland. For six weeks I had to do nothing but rest and should have really gone to a convalescent home at Stockport but the doctor said I could do this at home if I wanted to, which I did.

I missed out on the Coronation celebrations including the big bonfire and barbeque that was held on top of the Helm.

Things became a lot easier regarding work as we now had a proper workshop at home and could do our own repairs, saving both time and

Jack Dawson's (Steve Hawes uncle) Blacksmith's Shop (middle) in Longpool Kendal prior to it being knocked down (now Parker and Parker). On the left of it was Procter's pie and cake shop. *Steve Hawes*

Dad driving up the Helm on the International W6 with a load of branches for the Coronation bonfire.

The bonfire on the right. Standing left to right Jim Frearson, Jimmy Edmondson, Edwin Howson, Libby Moffat, Billy Brown, Mrs Keasey, Alan and Arthur Brown. Back row: Peter Bowden, Johnny Walker Keith Hine, Audrey Moffat, Jack Howson and dad, Jack Moffat.

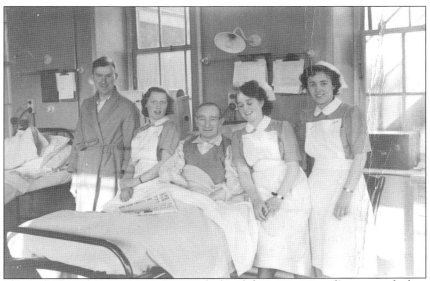

The medical ward I was in – me lying on bed on left. Mr Bowe standing next to bed and last two nurses are Jean Trevaskis and Ruth Ibbotson.

money. The large five bay open shed, housed the equipment and later we put two doors on two of the bays for our workshop. If there were jobs to be done like welding we used to take them to Jack Dawson's Blacksmith's shop on Longpool, Kendal, (now Parker and Parker) before we had our own welder. My friend Steve Hawes worked there (for 25 years), together with Alan Ellwood (Bense) from Ambleside and Bill Cragg who shoed all the horses. Bill also played the drums in a dance band. Dawson's were later taken over by Furmanite, a large firm that is still on Shap Road. We did not use our own local Smithy as it just mainly shoed horses. We used to go to Andrew Brown's, Auto Electrical Engineers, Wildman Street (now gone) and they repaired starters and dynamos as well as selling batteries amongst other things. George Addy was a fitter and diesel maintenance engineer and they had the first building on Mintsfeet Trading Estate, off Shap Road, Kendal in 1957. Fina Fuels supplied the fuel tanks and these were put onto stands. We had quite a job getting them into position and had to use wooden planks, wire ropes and two tractors – quite a task! (Fina Fuels was behind what is now Mint Motors).

I did not go back to school after I had made a full recovery as I was now fifteen and eligible to leave anyway. So happily I started working with dad even though the doctor had advised I should take a lighter job. I didn't heed his advice as this was the type of work that I had always known from a lad and never thought about doing anything else – I was Jack's lad – a chip of the old block.

In 1954 dad bought a Fordson Major tractor petrol TVO from Edwin Penny, a tractor dealer in Fowl Ing Lane, Kendal who had in turn obtained it from a dealer in Wiltshire. This was better equipped with hydraulics. We later fitted it with a Perkins L4 diesel engine that made it both economical and more powerful. The TVO (Tractor Vaporising Oil) tractors were now dying out.

Ernie Edwards who lived at 1 West View, Natland, had been a tractor driver in the War Ag and now drove for British Road Services (BRS – nationalised in 1950s). He kept his wagon, a Seddon 4-wheeler, in our yard between 1953-57. He used to cart pig iron from Millom Ironworks to the steel works at Scunthorpe. He later got an 8-wheeler Leyland Octopus wagon and carted railway lines that were made by British Steel in Workington to London. Sometimes I would go with him. During the winter months he would be on Shap patrol assisting (repairs etc) any BRS wagons that required it.

In 1954 Kendal experienced a very bad flood and K' Shoes evacuated all their workers and this also affected a lot of Kendal. Dad had unfortunately left his thresher parked on New Road, so he and mum tried to go over Romney footbridge but could not get any further because of all the water between there and Netherfield. They did however manage to get it moved all right to Natland and safety. Water was running for three days through our yard, this was the excess rainwater coming of Helm.

Due to repeated flooding in Kendal a scheme was implemented in 1971, involving the widening and deepening of the river in certain places. From Low Mills down to Netherfield Bridge a new retaining wall was built. The riverbed in some places was limestone and when the river was deepened this was pulled out with a caterpillar tractor and a tipper and some went for walling and others in people's rockeries. A large quantity of old bottles was discovered in a Victorian rubbish tip on the riverbank near the sewage works on Wattsfield. In the middle of writing this Kendal has experienced yet again flood conditions on Tuesday 3 February 2004 – some fifty years later but thanks to the flood defence scheme implemented in 1971 and with the rain finally subsiding after more than 24 hrs continuous rainfall, damage was limited and once again Kendal breathed a heavy sigh of relief!

Back now to farming. We cut hay on most of the farms in and around the Natland area and today a lot of these farms have now disappeared eg Jack Howson who farmed at Greenside next to the school. His land

Romney footbridge during the flood in December 1954. *Margaret Duff Collection*

became incorporated in the new school and swallowed up in other farms round about. I will just quickly run through who was there then.

Billy Rigg owned Newlands House on the Sedgwick road and he had a confectionary business in Kendal with two shops. He also kept pigs and Jim Armer, who was a bit of a character – a happy go lucky sort of chap – used to look after them as well as doing a lot of gardening work in the village.

J. Howson and Sons were poultry farmers at Newlands and they reared day old chicks. They had two sons, Edwin and Sydney and a daughter called Margery. They had sixteen acres of land and we had the job in summer of spreading the hen manure, it could be pretty potent at times with all the ammonia, especially in hot weather. Sydney was the first lad from Natland to be called up in the Second World War – he was only nineteen at the time.

Dixon Fox owned Larkrigg then and this was a big farm growing a lot of corn, turnips and mangels for cattle feed. Dixon often wore a Harris Tweed jacket and brown boots and he would bring his milk along to the milk stand for collection and as he was unable to back a tractor and trailer, he would go into one gate and out the other! The milk stand (concrete) was a communal one at the top of Hawes Lane just outside Natland Hall and is still there today. This was where all the farmers would bring their milk to be collected by Barnes & Nelson or R.O. Hodgson's of Milnthorpe and taken to Libby's milk factory, near Milnthorpe (now gone). The farmers usually had a good old crack (chat) there on a morning!

Jack Hook farmed at Cracalt Farm and Bob Hewitson used to work for him and lived in the village. Jack was very good with a gun and did a lot of competition clay pigeon shooting. He also helped out a lot with the annual sports held at Natland Park. He left to farm at Abbey Flats, near Calder Bridge, West Cumberland in 1968.

Harry Howson (not related to other Howson's and was from Yorkshire) owned Cracalt Farm and Cracalt House in the 1920s and was a timber merchant. At that time horses were used for snigging (hauling) out the wood and pulling the wood wagons. If they had to travel a long distance to a job the horses would be loaded on the back of a train at Oxenholme Station and taken as near as possible to where they wanted to be.

During the war an old bus body stood on the hill at Larkrigg and was used as an observation post. The men who manned it worked two hours

Left: Stramongate, Kendal during the flood in December 1954. *Margaret Duff Collection*

Margaret Addison (later to marry Pearson Charnley) at Crow Park, Natland in the cornfield in the early 1940s.

Dad driving his International Standard tractor cutting corn with a self-binder for Jack Howson at Broadflats, near Helme Lodge in 1954.

on and two hours off. In wartime Bob Airey was farmer at Higher House Farm, he was also a butcher. The house was half in Natland and half in Sedgwick, as the boundary was said to run through the middle. Later Billy Walling came to farm there until he retired in the 1980s when it ceased to be a farm.

Bob Addison of Crow Park (now a private house), just down the lane from us, was Margaret Charnley's father's farm – and Jim her brother became a builder and lived at Oxenholme. Margaret later married Pearson who helped build our house and has always lived near us.

Eddie Moorhouse and his son Dennis farmed at High House Farm, Helm Lane and they had at one time a milk round in and around Natland and Oxenholme. Dennis played the accordion in a 1940s dance band called 'Mayfair'. Also in the band was Jack Bennett on drums, Mary Allen on piano and Colin Dixon on the accordion. All except Colin Dixon were from Natland and they used to play in the old school at Natland and locally at village halls in Sedgwick, Staveley, Levens, Windermere and many other villages.

Bill Howson farmed at Natland Abbey and was then an old chap ready for retirement. Old Bob Bindloss lived in Oxenholme Lane and he had buildings below Higher House (now a Barn conversion) and a lot of land behind the present school. During the Second World War he would take his milk to Oxenholme Station and this was loaded onto the milk train that travelled down to Liverpool.

Dobson (Dobbie) Nelson farmed at Brow Head Farm – a fairly new farm just down from Oxenholme Lane junction with the A65. This is no longer a farm and the house is now rented. The new hospital, Westmorland General, and Asda superstore are now built on his land.

Jack Howson farmed at Greenside, now gone (above the school) and had land on Broadflats, Natland Road (¼ a mile along on the left). Jack lived in the house next to the new school (Oxenholme Lane). He smoked black twist and wore knee length breeches and had the nickname of 'Timber' as he was very tall.

The biggest farm was Natland Hall and that was farmed by Johnny Dodgson and is still run today by his two sons Robert and John. Johnny did a bit of cattle dealing. He had two men working for him, Arthur Cheeseman (who also worked for the War Ag) and big John Chapman. In 1969 Johnny contacted me to say that a cow had fallen into a six-foot brick culvert at Cracalt in the field above the canal and it had been missing for several days. We rigged up a harness underneath its body and winched the cow out with a tractor and loader. Thankfully it was none the worse of the ordeal and managed to walk away though somewhat stiffly (gingerly)!

Mr Metcalfe had Riggs Gardens which was on Natland Road, in the three cornered field midway on the right between Natland and Kendal. He had greenhouses on this and we ploughed the land where he grew mainly flowers and vegetables.

Natland Park, just out of Natland, was farmed by Edward Kendal. I remember he always wore brown bib and brace overalls and always had shinny brown leather boots. Sports Day was always held there every year and was always as near the 20th June as possible. We used to help to put the ropes up for the ring. The events included a fell race that took in the Helm and some of the fell runners then were: Jonathon Gibson from Burneside; Keith Clements from Kendal; Bill Teasdale from Caldbeck and Gordon Wilkinson from Rusland. There was also Cumberland and Westmorland Wrestling – Wilf Brocklebank from Tewitfield; Ted Dunlinson from West Cumberland; Jim Bland from Arnside Tower and John and Robin Richardson from Laverock Bridge. There was also a motorcycle grass track and I remember Jimmy Cannon from Natland used to take part. There were also hounds trails and flat races together with the usual beer tent and bookies. It was popular but in the 1950s for one reason or another it moved to Barrows Green and was there for a few years before it finally wound up.

Natland Millbeck Farm was owned by the Crewdson family and Jack Gorst was farm manager when we first did work on the farm. He had two sons, Malcolm and Gordon. John Gardner came to work for the Colonel in 1953 and took over the farm himself in the early 1970s. There was an old corn mill just below the farm – now converted to a house. There were about six families living in the cottages, one was Hubert Williamson's and his father before him was gardener at Helme Lodge. Years later when having a crack with John Gardner one day, I brought up the subject matter of holidays and asked him, 'Where are you going on holiday?' He replied, 'Nay I don't go on holiday Billy, I would rather do a bit of muck spreading!'

Now back to the village itself, the blacksmith's shop was next to Smithy Buildings on Sedgwick Road, Natland and in 1910 when they were building the new church John Dixon, the blacksmith, had the job at night of sharpening the chisels and walling hammers ready for the workers in the morning. Years later Richard 'Dickie' Mitchell who was blacksmith at Ghyll Mill, New Hutton (1946-52) would spend two days a

Eddie Moorhouse, High House,
Natland with two Clydesdale
horses in 1932. *Dennis Moorhouse*

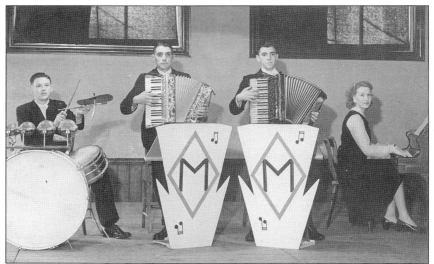

The Mayfair Band at Burneside village hall in 1944-5. Left to right is Jack Bennett,
Dennis Moorhouse, Colin Dixon and Mary Allen. *Dennis Moorhouse*

John Gardner,
Natland Millbeck
Farm in 1964 with
his two dogs Judy
and Gyp.

Dickie Mitchell, seen here at Crosthwaite Smithy shoeing 'Sheila' in June 1965.
Elizabeth Mitchell

week at Natland shoeing horses. He then went to Crosthwaite where his family still carry on the business today.

Billy Douthwaite was an extremely tall man measuring in at 7' 2" to be precise and was born in Barrow and lived at Green Tree House in 1911. He worked at the iron works in Barrow and was said to do the work of two men carrying pig iron and got paid accordingly (two men's wages!). He only lived to the age of forty-six.

Dick Holmes nurseries (now Holmes Nurseries) were just a small concern then with just the gardens up near the bungalow (beside the new school) and about two acres of land on Sedgwick Road (now the nursery) that we used to plough. They had a small shop (converted from a house) just of the Green where they sold vegetables.

The post office was once a pub – The Horse and Farrier – but was closed in the late 1800s because of rowdiness! When we came the postmaster was Mr Broadbent who ran it with his wife. Mrs Broadbent is still living in Natland and is one of the oldest residents. Nowadays Graham Needham has it as a shop as well.

Quite a lot of people went to the Church in Natland. Mum was a big church goer and used to go every Sunday but my sisters and I would go about once a month if I was not helping dad. Rev. Mars was the vicar then. I was later confirmed at Milnthorpe Church in 1953.

The original school in Natland was next to the church. It was not a large school and in 1967 it was knocked down and replaced by the new church school in Oxenholme Lane. Three houses were built in the old site and the playground now forms their gardens.

Audrey my sister had a horse called Silver that she kept in a little field down Hawes Lane. On leaving school she worked in the Midland Bank in Kendal before going to work for Norman Croft's in Wildman Street. She later married Ian Dunn who had two electrical shops, one in Kendal (corner of Maude Street/Stricklandgate) and the other in Kirkby Stephen. They have a son and a daughter, Jonathan and Bronwen. Audrey and Ian are now retired and live at Wheatstone, Preston Patrick.

My other sister Libby left school in 1955 and went to work in the Provincial Insurance Company, Kendal. Then later she worked in stables at Bletchley, Buckinghamshire looking after horses. After this she came back to Kendal to work in the Radiology Department at Westmorland County Hospital. She married in 1965, had two sons, Jason and Harvey, and now lives in Fort William.

Early picture of the old village school and church on the Green at Natland. *Margaret Duff Collection*

Sawing wood at Laverock Bridge Farm, near Kendal in 1954. Noel and Robin Richardson with dad.

Dick Holmes of Holmes Nursery in the 1950s. *Ronnie Holmes*

Back to contracting – we used to keep busy during the winter doing various jobs – muck spreading, sawing wood and snow ploughing for the council.

We had a Massey Harris muck spreader and the muck was loaded on with a fork – there were no loaders then. I loaded one side and dad the other. Quite often in those days a dead hen would come flying out the back of the spreader and hit you on the back, uph! I used to hate it when that happened. The smelly end of the midden was always where they had emptied the earth closets (toilets). It was a great day when dad let me take a load out and spread it – I remember the feeling as if it was yesterday!

Another job father did during winter was sawing up firewood for various farms. He would go along on his old Fordson tractor, with his mobile saw bench on the back of the trailer and on getting there it would be lifted down onto the ground and connected to the pulley belt of the tractor. The farmers would have a pile of branches sawn into manageable lengths from what had been blown down the previous winter, together with a pile of old fencing posts stacked in the stack yard, ready to be sawn up into this winter's supply of firewood for the house. It would be put into the woodshed (stick house) to dry out, ready for the farmer's wife to carry into the house in an old swill basket. Any straight pieces of larch would be made into fencing posts and rails – nothing was ever wasted and everything put to its best possible use.

Snow ploughing for the Council was another job we did. They had a Depot at Sedgwick just past the entrance to Sedgwick House. They would fit the metal plough on the front of our tractor and we would clear the roads round about and would go as far as Killington. They would usually ring us – otherwise we would just use our own discretion. We covered the surrounding area – Natland, Sedgwick, Hincaster, Levens, Brigsteer, Crosthwaite and back round to Killington. The Council just did the main roads in those days – that was just snow ploughing as they did not use much salt then.

In the 1950s we obtained the contract from Nuttalls, Civil Engineers just off Longpool, for ploughing and reseeding on the new pipe track (water pipe for Manchester Corporation) from Selside to Mealbank. They fenced ten foot either side of the pipe (called easement), and in total the track would be roughly thirty-five feet wide. The pipes were cast iron, four foot in diameter and put about eight feet deep. One day a dumper truck went over and rolled down the hill – luckily the driver escaped uninjured. This water was piped all the way from Haweswater to Manchester. The original pipe laying began in 1950 and was completed in 1956. Eric Bryers was a linesman at that time and worked for Manchester Corporation for 33 years before retiring as an inspector.

In 1956 dad and I were working for Windermere Council reseeding the Glebe on Bowness, when the film 'Dambusters' was being made and we had a great time watching the Lancaster bombers flying low over the lake – it was a spectacular sight!

I went ploughing with dad to Lance Wharton's at Sunbiggin, near Orton Scar. Some of this fell land was covered with heather and was done with a single furrow plough. Sometimes we ploughed up empty shell cases from the Second World War as the army had tanks in the area of Orton Scar and you can still see the tank tracks today.

Cutting corn with a self-binder could be a difficult job if it was very laid (lying flat on the ground – caused by the weather or a very heavy crop) and had to be cut one way, then stooked some days later. Afterwards it could either be threshed and baled off the field or carted in by tractor and trailer and stacked in the farmyard in ricks (stack yard). At the Martins farm, Helsington Laithes, it was very flat down by the river and we always threshed and baled it off the fields.

In 1956 another tractor was bought from Norman Croft's in Wildman Street, this was another new Fordson Major diesel costing £650 on the road. As hay time was becoming more automated we bought our second pick-up baler so that we could both bale at different farms. We also ran

Natland in 1958 showing the road criss-crossing the Green. Church View in the foreground, Natland Hall Farm just behind and just beyond at the tree is our bungalow. *Bobby Dodgson*

Top: Jimmy Lancaster from Low Sizergh Farm, near Kendal, busy taking part in Farleton Ploughing Match in 1954. Also in the picture are, on the right hand-side of tractor wheel; George Park, Deepslack Farm, Whinfell; Danny Jackson (wearing berry) from Derby Arms Farm; next to him two Henderson brothers from Lane End Farm, Brigsteer; Edwin Ellis and his son Brian from Lane Foot Farm, Kendal.
Jimmy Lancaster/Westmorland Gazette

Left: Ernest Ireland's 21st party, in 1956, in the old school hall taken by the Westmorland Gazette.
1st table left – me, Geoff Wightman; Eunis Garnett; Brian Holmes; Libby Moffat; George Holmes; …? ; Dennis Moorhouse and Bob Bindloss.
1st table right – Peter Bowden (front middle); Margaret and Alan Robson; …?..:
Joe Richardson; Audrey Moffat; Johnny Walker; Mary Atkinson and John Atkinson.
Back table (l to r) – Danny Proctor; Mrs Ewing; Ernest Ireland's cousin; Christine Crabtree and Geoff Scott.
3rd table left – Bill Hall and wife; dad – Jack Moffat; Margaret and Pearson Charnley; ? Brian Johnston.
3rd table right – Fred Scott; Marta George (Italian); Geoff George; …? ,
Jimmy Cannon – with Mrs Scott serving on.

two mowing machines with cutter bars and later as already mentioned drum mowers came in.

All meals were provided in those days. In the morning the farmer's wife came out with a basket and can of tea, this was what we called bagging or drinking. Dinnertime was always at half past twelve and teatime at four when we had bread and jam or cheese and cake.

Prizet Farm was rented to Walter Wightman. He had four sons, Derek, Douglas, Geoff and Dennis. While dad was ploughing there I would play with Geoff in the early days. Dennis later did medal ploughing with horses. In 1957 Lancaster's came to Prizet Farm and farmed for the next twenty years. Jimmy Lancaster went to school with me and he also did medal ploughing but with a Fordson Major and drag or trailer plough and later hydraulic. Competition ploughing was held at various farms around Farleton, Arnside, Sedbergh, Silverdale and Ellel, near Galgate, Lancaster, where they are still held.

Short's factory at Troutbeck Bridge was where the Sunderland Flying Boats were built during the Second World War. Bungalows were built for the workers near Culgarth Farm. After the factory closed the prefabs were pulled down and the land reverted back into fields. In 1956 I did all the ploughing, about ten acres and all sorts of debris came up. Prisoners from Bela River Camp near Milnthorpe came by wagon and I drove the tractor and trailer while they filled it. They brought sandwiches with them. The bread I remember was very thick and filled with either jam or cheese.

I started going to motorbike scrambles with dad in 1949. He had a 500 cc Matchless in those days. It was black with a black and chrome tank with a large M. Father would wear a great coat, goggles (Mark Eights) made then of leather and glass, cloth cap (no helmets then) leggings and wellingtons if very wet. I used to wear an oilskin coat and leggings, balaclava, goggles and wellingtons.

The scrambles were seasonal starting about October and going right through to February or March. We went to scrambles at Low Lindeth Farm, near Bowness; Plumpton and Lazonby, both near Penrith. Locally at Helsington (grass tracks as well) – this was opposite the Shenstone Hotel, on Helsington Laithes Farm, owned by the Stricklands of Sizergh and rented then to Walter Martin. Walter's son Derek was a scramble rider in the 1960s. The first scramble held there was in 1954 but stopped in 1969. This was because the new Kendal By-Pass was being built and access would have proved difficult if not dangerous. For the next two

Right: Scrambling in the early 1950s at Brown Rigg Fell, Plumpton, near Penrith. *Margaret Duff Collection*

years grass tracks took place at Wilkinson's of High Foulshaw Farm, near Gilpin Bridge. All the scrambles finished more or less in the 1950s.

The scrambles as a rule started about lunchtime, though the morning was always taken up with practising. There were different classes of bikes, though mostly 350 cc and 500 cc, all four strokes and British made. There were no two-stroke scramble bikes then. The bikes would arrive either in the back of a van or a trailer pulled by a car. Some would even ride their bikes there and just take the number plates of and put their racing number on.

When going to Penrith we would maybe set off about nine o'clock on a Sunday morning and take our sandwiches and flask in a bag that I would have on my back. We sometimes would meet up with some friends at the Duke of Cumberland and set off together. We would be there all day finishing about four o'clock. There would be about twenty or so bikes taking part, each winning their own heats and going through to the final. It was always a good day out and we would meet other people we knew there.

When we went to Lindeth we would go in the car sometimes with mum and dad and maybe one of my friends. We would take a picnic and mum would usually go for a walk and leave us lads to watch the scramble.

Some of the riders were John Airey, Smoky Dawson (Far Sawrey), Billy Milburn (Windermere), Alan Tatham (Natland) and his brother Hughie (Windermere), Zeke Myers (Langdale) on his Flying Saucer, Jackie Foster (Dalston), Tommy Moffat (Sedbergh – my uncle), Billy Tiffin, Les Pickthall, Foster Williams, Percy Harris – Kendal lads – as well as Cecil O'Loughlin, who owned the BSA agency in Kendal, his garage and showroom were just below the Woolpack. James Walker motorcycles sold AJS and Matchless, and Gilly (Gilbert Parkinson) was Ariel agent.

Note the unusual name of Flying Saucer given to Zeke Myers' Norton motorcycle. This came about as he had bought the bike from Dr Derbyshire and his son had reputedly seen a flying saucer and the item was mentioned in the Gazette at the time.

Today there is still a classic known as the Nostalgic Scramble held in September annually at Middleton, near Sedbergh.

8692

WESTMORLAND MOTOR CLUB

LAFONE SCRAMBLE

FOR SOLO MOTOR CYCLES

A.C.U. PERMIT No. A.40.
T.T.C. No. 455.

LOW LINDETH FARM, WINSTER

Near Windermere

SUNDAY, 7th AUGUST, 1949.

Starting at 2-30 p.m.

Official Programme — Price One Shilling

Officials:

JUDGE and HANDICAPPER : J. H. LAFONE, Esq.
Timekeepers : F. RITCHEN and J. WOODBURN.
Lap Scorers : D. MALLINSON, S. COUTTS, O. L. BANKS.
Starter and Competitors' Marshal : L. M. GORTON.
Paddock and Equipment Marshals : P. VOGT and E. J. HOLYOAKE.
Chief Marshal and Clerk of the Course : Mr. W. J. MONTGOMERY.
Chief Car Park Stewards : Mr. and Mrs. G. GRISDALE and Mr. F. W. TYSON.
Chief Programme Stewards: G. W. DODDS and F. BRENNAND.
Scoreboard Marshal : B. A. CRABTREE.
Travelling Marshals : R. SIMPSON, G. LLOYD and R. NICHOLSON.

Course Marshals
R. M. MOSER, M. WATSON, N. JACKSON, B. CARTER, D. PERRIN,
A. WILLIAMS, A. WRIGHT, N. F. PHILLIPSON, R. D. HUMBER, N.
O'LOUGHLIN, J. COLLINSON, H. D. BUCHANAN, N. WHITEHEAD, J. AIREY,
G. DUGDALE, E. SIMPSON, H. SHELTON and CLUB MEMBERS of the
NORTHERN CENTRAL.

A.C.U. Steward : J. WILSON.

Sportscasting by W. ASPINWALL, Windermere.

Hon. Treasurer : G. W. DODDS, 22, Kendal Green, Kendal.
Hon. Trials Secretary : L. M. GORTON, 19, Church Street, Windermere.

DONATIONS FROM PROCEEDS TO LOCAL CHARITIES.

Note the Date of our NEXT SCRAMBLE : 11th SEPT.

Westmorland Gazette, Ltd., Printers, Kendal.

Event 4.—LAFONE SCRAMBLE

UNLIMITED C.C. RACE

First Five in each Heat Ride in Final.

(Heats 3 Laps; Final 12 Laps)

HEAT 1

1.	W. H. Millburn	Windermere	348 c.c. B.S.A.
7.	J. Forster	Dalston	249 c.c. Velocette
20.	P. Harris	Kendal	347 c.c. Matchless
19.	J. K. Hirst	Bradford	348 c.c. B.S.A.
24.	A. A. Todd	Kendal	348 c.c. Velocette
35.	M. Tyson	Windermere	347 c.c. A.J.S.
6.	J. Bowerbank	Carlisle	347 c.c. A.J.S.
2.	P. Roberts	Barrow	348 c.c. B.S.A.
17.	A. Curtiss	Bradford	500 c.c. Norton
32.	M. T. Wilkinson	Bradford	498 c.c. Triumph
40.	Mac Davidson	Penrith	348 c.c. B.S.A.
5.	W. A. Smith	Kendal	246 c.c. Matchless
22.	W. Philip	Kendal	347 c.c. A.J.S.
31.	A. R. Eastwood	Morecambe	348 c.c. B.S.A.
45.	W. T. Hardman	Ulverston	249 c.c. Velocette
47.	J. Clark	Barrow	349 c.c. Velocette
50.	A. Tatham	Natland	347 c.c. A.J.S.
53.	G. Clayton	Kendal	347 c.c. Matchless

1st. *Percy* 2nd. *1* 3rd. *19* 4th. *35* 5th. *7*

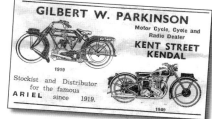

Items of interest out of the
Lafone Scramble
programme 1949.
John Bethall

Highgate, Kendal in the 1950s *Margaret Duff Collection*

VII

Growing up and flying the Nest

I WAS REALLY ENJOYING LIFE, though working for dad could be quite gruelling but I learnt a lot and enjoyed going out with my friends. On Sunday nights we used to ride round town on our motorbikes – BSA, Matchless, Nortons, Triumphs speed-twins (nothing much has changed – apart from youngsters now in cars) calling at Tognorelli's (Gianni's – Italian restaurant), in Stramongate for coffee. I have seen as many as 25–30 motorbikes parked outside.

My first motorbike I got in 1954 was a Francis Barnett, 197 cc, bought privately. Tognorelli's (Togs) was a family run café that was very popular with the youngsters in those days, it was counter service and you could get hot Vimto in winter and coffee, tea or such like. There was always a nice coal fire there on cold winter days to warm you up after being on the bike. I also had a 350 cc AJS and Matchless 500 cc – I stopped riding (1957) after the sad loss of two uncles who died as the result of motor cycle accidents.

Lads in those days used to work up to owning a car by starting off with purchasing the small motorbikes – 125 cc e.g. BSA Bantam (no Japanese then), Excelsior and James, then progressed up to 250, 350 and 500. The makes then that were popular were AJS, Matchless, Ariel, BSA. James Walker, Rose and Crown Works, Stricklandgate (the yard is part of Wainwrights Yard and Daniel Gray the hairdresser has the building) was the AJS and Matchless agent. Cecil O'Loughlin, had BSA road and scramble bikes and his shop was on Stricklandgate, just below the Woolpack Hotel. Gilly Parkinson, along with selling a lot of pushbikes was also the main Ariel dealer in Kent Street, (now a nightclub) Kendal. Lads progressed from them into vans – Morris 1000 and Mini were the most popular then. Girls on the other hand mostly had scooters before saving up to buy their first car. The thing was mobility to get you about. You learnt a lot, you took a pride in your first vehicles and worked on them to keep them roadworthy. We mostly did our own maintenance learning

The Four Musketeers! Standing in front of Alan's Austin A35 – (l to r) me, Steve Hawes, Peter Kirk and Alan Brown in our yard in 1961.

from each other and our dads if they had bikes and cars. Nobody really had a lot of money in those days.

On Friday nights in winter during the mid 1950s we went to dances in the country, to. Burton, Staveley, Crook and Witherslack and usually called at the local pub on the way. I usually went with Alan Brown, Michael Tyson, Steve Hawes and Hanson Charnley. We sometimes got home very late.

Bowness dances on a Saturday night were held in the Embassy Ballroom. Sometimes about six of us would go up on the bus but we often missed the last one home – either stayed too long or had taken a girl home. One night I had been out to the wee small hours, it was when I had been driving and had taken a girl back to her house then picked up the rest of my mates who had started walking home. The lack of sleep caught up with me the following day while ploughing at Staveley. I parked up to have my dinner behind this wall and promptly dropped off to sleep. I had to return the following day to finish the job – dad was not best pleased! We also went to the Parish Hall at Kendal on Saturday nights and that was another favourite. I started going when I was about sixteen years old, suit and tie was the order of the day on a Saturday night, dancing to waltzes, Foxtrot and generally shuffling round as best we could. All the girls would sit up the sides of the room and the blokes would stand at the bottom weighing up the form. There were quite a few local dance bands in those days and two that played at the Parish Hall were Brian Coulter's and Five Kings. Brian played drummer, Harry Stock was double base and G. Middleton played trumpet. In Five Kings there were – Duggie Phillips played drums; Harry Stock – double base; C Raffles – piano; J. Parker – clarinet; J. May – trumpet and F. Marsden – trombone. It will be noted that there were more than five in the band and some played in both!

If you didn't go dancing on a Saturday night you would maybe go to the cinema – there were three in Kendal then. The Palladium on Sandes Avenue (now County Mews – apartments); Roxy (near where the Telecom is on Sandes Ave/Blackhall Rd) and St George's, (now houses) Stramongate. All these have now gone.

The bike test I remember was a fairly simple test I took in Kendal. The tester would just watch that you gave the correct hand signals (no indicators on bikes then). I learned to drive the car with my father in our Morris Ten. If we were going to a job my father would let me drive so I got a lot of practise and of course I had been driving a tractor for years before that. I also had lessons from a Major Hine who lived just off Sedbergh Road and used either his car or dad's. I passed my test in 1957 during the Suez crisis.

The foyer area of St George's Theatre, Kendal – where you had to queue for the next house. *Margaret Duff Collection*

A great event in my life was in 1957 when I got my Morris Eight van, this was an ex-Post Office van and it gave me a bit more freedom to travel about. The vans were advertised in the Gazette and dad and me went round to the GPO Depot behind the Post Office in Stricklandgate, saw them and put in a tender for one. I paid £100 for it and of course it was red so I sprayed it grey and black – two tone. It was very fashionable in those days – top half was black. It was only 800 cc but it could go fast in a prevailing wind! It was also used for work for transporting bits and pieces between jobs.

Shortly afterwards Alan Brown and I decided to take a trip to Devon. We travelled eight hundred miles, camping at various places. We had primus stove, tent and sleeping bags, though half the time we slept in the van as it was raining or we were unfit. I remember well a night in Clovelly where we got legless on scrumpy (cider), pitching our tent that night proved impossible so we slept in the van. Porlock Hill was 1 in 3 and was very hard work for the little Morris. This was Alan's turn to drive that day and I had the arduous task of getting out and giving it a push. It was a good holiday and the van served us well on our travels.

One night for a bet Alan and me went over Romney footbridge in his Austin 7. We managed no problem! The footbridge was taken down in 1989 to make way for the new Romney Road bridge that was finished two months early on 18 December 1990 and in celebration of this was decorated with Christmas decorations. A few years later the footbridge was re-erected this time across the railway line between Beezon and Mintsfeet Industrial Estates to give pedestrian access (short cut) between the two estates.

Me and the lads used to go into Woolworths in Kendal on a Saturday afternoon during winter time after finishing work. We would go in for a look around and would maybe buy bits and pieces but if truth be known, we only went to have a look at the girls. I was nineteen and the rest of the lads would be about the same age. This day I saw this rather attractive girl who had a nice twinkle in her eyes. I went in a few more Saturdays before I finally plucked up courage to ask her out. Her name was Mavis Burrows and she lived in Underley Road, with her mum, dad and two brothers, Raymond and John. She was working in Woolworths on a Saturday to earn extra money for Christmas. She said, 'Yes, she would like to go out with me,' and that was the start of our courting days. I think our first date was to the pictures on the following Saturday night. Though I must admit that not all nights out ran smoothly, as they were ruled by my work, which depended a lot on the weather and I often turned up late for the

Me and Mavis on our wedding day standing outside St Thomas's Church.
Frederick Thwaites

pictures or if we made it, I sometimes slept through the film. At that time Mavis was working at Atkinson and Griffins garage, next to Crabtrees, in Kirkland, Kendal as a typist. Later she worked at Norweb, the electricity board in Parkside Road, and later up at their offices at Castle Green.

When we all started courting, (now I think it's called 'an item') our social life settled down into a pattern. On Saturday nights our favourite meeting place was the cocktail bar in the Woolpack Hotel (now a fast food restaurant). From there we would go up the Lakes for a meal, to the pictures, or down to Morecambe with our respective girlfriends, Alan Brown in his Austin Seven (he had this before his van) and me in my Morris van. Some regular calling places were the Hydro and Stags at Bowness, Newby Bridge Hotel and the Beech Hill. Dances at Warton Grange were also popular. At Morecambe it would be the Broadway where you could have Cornish pasties, pickled eggs and jars of mussels. Another pub was the Golden Bowl at Overton, nicknamed 'Snatchums', when the tide was high you could be marooned and have to wait till it went out again. Dances at the pier in Morecambe where we danced to some good dance bands including Joe Loss.

In the late 1950s we went with two friends Mike and Sylvia Tyson and toured Scotland in the little Morris, we covered eleven hundred miles visiting Edinburgh and the Highlands. The roads were very narrow and had passing places. Bed and breakfast was about 10 shillings (50p) per night and most of our other meals we cooked on a little primus stove.

Tony Wilson who then lived at Natland Park was courting Celia Thompson (later married) who lived on Kendal Green and were good friends. Mavis and I were married at St Thomas's Church Kendal in 1960 and went on honeymoon touring Devon and Cornwall. We lived to begin with in Natland Hall farm cottage in the farmyard – only small with a bed-sit and kitchen. My wages then were £10 a week.

In the late 1950s-60s I used to go as a spectator to motorcycle races at Oulton Park in Cheshire. AJS, Norton, Matchless, MV Agusta and Gilera (Italian) being raced – Japanese bikes had not come on the scene.

In 1960 Alan and I decided to go for the weekend to Scarborough Motor Cycle Races at Olivers Mount. Scarborough was what they called a mini T. T. as this is quite a hilly course with a lot of hairpin bends. It was a three-mile single-track course. There was a meeting in July but the main one was in September and two or three thousand people usually went. There were a lot of heats starting with a 125 cc, 250 cc, 350 cc and 500 cc, with about 12 riders in each heat. There were also races for sidecar outfits or chairs as they were sometimes called!

We left on the Friday night about 6 o'clock in Alan's brand new grey Austin A35 van that he received as a 21st present from his grandfather who bought it from Lakeland Garage, in Sandes Avenue, Kendal. The registration number was HEC 21. We went via Sedbergh, Hawes, Leyburn, Thirsk and just as we were going over Sutton Bank I could smell something burning. We stopped to check and lifted the bonnet and the paint was frizzling on the cylinder head – you could fry an egg on it! We arrived about 9pm to our digs at a small boarding house. We got washed and changed, then went out and got fish and chips, bread and butter at a café. Afterwards we went for a walk up the prom and then went for a drink before retiring for the night.

Next morning we were up bright and early for breakfast and went to the race track about nine o'clock to see them practising. Alan Shepherd was the rider we had come to see, he was a local lad from Grange-over-Sands and was related to Alan's brother-in-law. It had been arranged that we were going to be able to meet him in the pits together with some of the other riders and of course have a look at their motorbikes – so we were very excited. We met Bob McIntyre from Glasgow; John Hartle (later killed); John Surtees and Derek Minter. Alan Shepherd was a nice chap, tall and fair haired. Bikes were transported there in vans. We had met previously and he made us very welcome. Alan was busy preparing his bikes so we gladly gave him a hand doing an oil change. He had two motorbikes an AJS 7R 350 cc and a Matchless G50 500 cc. Between races we also helped him to prepare the bike for the next race. We would oil the rear chain, clean the air filter, fly screen and generally give the bike a good clean over – so it looked good! We also did some lap boarding – so the riders knew which lap they were on. I think he won the 350 cc race and second in the 500 cc. That evening the trophies were presented and we left for our homeward journey after a lovely weekend.

Alan Shepherd became a works MZ rider, these were made in East Germany and when he got a new bike he had to meet them on the border. His riding days sadly came to an end when he had a bad accident whilst testing a Honda in Italy and he never rode again.

Penningtons Quarry 1957–58

Busy unloading lime. Dad at the back of a Bedford TK tipped up and lime being loaded via an elevator onto spreader with Fordson Major tractor. This was at Kirkby Lonsdale in 1964–65.

VIII

Lime Spreading

IN 1956 WE STARTED SPREADING LIME for Pennington's Lime Works (now the Council Rubbish Tip off the Underbarrow road), Kendal and had an eight-year contract with them. The previous contractor's contract had come to an end and the traveller Jack Williams asked if we would like to put our names forward for the contract. Pennington's was a large quarry in those days making bricks, chippings and burnt lime. We also spread rough lime dust from there.

John Gott was also a traveller who worked for Pennington's and went round the farms selling the lime. Jack used to drive a Standard Ten car and covered the Lakes and the Kendal area; and John in a Standard Ten van covered the southern end.

Lime was used to take the acidity out of the soil. It was also an important additive to your soil re your PH levels – if you had not enough lime on the ground other fertilisers would not work as well – there would be a chemical imbalance. The PH should read about 7.5. It was importantly so on arable farms that grew their own wheat and barley, if it had not been limed properly before seeding, the second year's crop yield could be down ten per cent or more. A lot of lime was required for growing root crops eg. kale, turnips, cabbages and sugar beat.

With Pennington's and also later with other companies that we were under contract to, we provided the equipment and they found us the work and we got paid so much a ton. In 1956 we were paid 7s. 6d. (38p) for spreading ground limestone and 10s. (50p) for kibbled (burnt) lime.

The wagons in those days carried five or six tons at a time and were ex-War Department Bedfords and Austins which were very heavy on petrol (only about 14 miles to the gallon). The others were Seddons, Morris Commercials and Leylands and these were all diesel. Some of the drivers who brought the lime to us were John Barker known as 'Trigger', Bill Rook known as 'Whacka', little Johnny Hodgson, George Steel (Geordy), Tommy Ronson, Horace Galloway, Norman Forsyth,

Bill Rowlinson, Billy Graham and Allen Carradice known as 'Crafty' was quite a character (over 65 when he gave up driving).

T. K. Robinson and Norman Wilson also spread lime in and around the same area as us and through lime merchants and feeding stuff firms. This was done mostly in the winter from October to November right through into spring when the weather was dry. We went all round the Lakes, Kirkby-in-Furness and Ulverston. You couldn't put kibbled lime (burnt with coke in a kiln then later oil-fired kiln) out when it was frosty as it used to cockle (go lumpy) and it wouldn't fall out properly. During the summer in the mid 1950s the Government gave the farmers a high subsidy of up to 75% to enable them to sell lime off-season. Then when the subsidy came of it the lime naturally dropped.

We usually put on two tons to the acre. When travelling to a farm the tractor pulled the lime spreader and the elevator. Some preferred the lime ramp – wagons reverse up and empty contents into the spreader. Pennington's would come with the lorries to the farm and we would spread at each farm. Each farm in those days would take 30-40 tons a time and then we would move onto the next farm.

There wasn't much traffic on the roads in those days. We would travel A6 then onto the A590 to Barrow and probably only see some heavy vehicles. It was a long way to Ulverston and Barrow and we would set off at 6 am and be back around 6 pm.

A farmer wanting lime up a steep hill once asked Allen Carradice if his wagon would go up? He said, 'No,' so the farmer replied, 'If I were to put a dozen eggs on that seat would it go up?' Allen replied, 'It would bloody fly up!'

We got more and more jobs so we employed two men. Colin Wharton (1956–57 came and stayed for about 4 years), from Tebay was a tractor driver and John Todd from Kendal drove the caterpillar spreader that was taken to the farms on a Seddon wagon with the lime spreader, the elevator towed behind. (We still had Jimmy Cross from Staveley (1950s) doing general contract work and later on the caterpillar; Derek Harbey was still part-time doing mostly grass cutting in summer and muck spreading in winter).

When I first started lime spreading I had never been much further afield than Milnthorpe on a tractor. One night dad said, 'Thou's garn to Ulverston tomorrow.' I was only eighteen years old and I felt as if I was going out into the big wide world. I learnt a lot by travelling about the countryside and met a lot of interesting people from all walks of life.

Tractors were bad to start on cold frosty mornings and this was due mainly to the wax in the diesel. To overcome this we would light a fire underneath the tractor to generate some heat round the diesel pipes and then tow them off with another vehicle.

It was a cold job in those days sitting on the tractor spreading lime as there were no heaters or cabs and I would get well wrapped up with a fur lined Davy Crocket hat, scarf, donkey jacket (very thick dark jacket) jeans or boiler suits and woolly gloves – but still managed to succumb to chilblains and kins (chapped – small cuts) on my hands. (Note: kibbled lime was nasty when it was wet it burnt your skin and in summer it did the same when you sweated). Sometimes if we could we would have our meals in an outbuilding and this was always that bit warmer if it was attached to the byre, as the heat being generated from the cattle was much appreciated. Other times when I was working in some wild places and there was no shelter, I would light a fire behind a wall to keep warm while eating. Sometimes you got so cold you would almost fall out of the tractor as all feeling had gone out of your legs. It was terrible at times!

By now we were working for a lot of firms and got plenty of work to keep us busy. We still received work from Penningtons but were also now under contract to Brunskill and Farrow Ltd, Kendal; Ramsdens Ltd of Preston; Jordans, Allhallows Lane, Kendal; Lunesdale Farmers; Cumberland and Westmorland Farmers; West Cumberland Farmers; Bradshaws of Kirkby Lonsdale and Furnace Supplies of Ulverston.

I remember during 1962–63 we were spreading lime near the estuary at Brook Holme Farm, Lancaster for Lunesdale Farmers. It was so foggy that I drove into a pond by accident getting well and truly stuck. It took two tractors to pull me out.

One farm I remember was way up the Trough of Bowland, a large sheep farm, with two thousand head of sheep and twelve sheepdogs. We spread about three hundred tons of lime and fifty tons of basic slag (£40 a ton hauled and spread), the going I remember was very soft and hilly. Basic slag used to come from the steelworks at Middlesbrough (lower grade) or Scunthorpe (higher grade). The farmer had to leave their stock off the land for a week to ten days until the rain had managed to wash it in.

We used to go down to Mr Lawson's at Bank End Farm, this was very low lying at Cockerham, near Garstang, and was tidal, so we had to wait for the tide to go out so that we could gain access to the farm. A new sea wall was later built to stop the land from flooding. The furthest south we went was to Myerscough College, near Blackpool. I remember seeing the sea frozen at Morecambe Promenade when I was going down to Overton, I was amazed, was a bit like being on Mars!

Another day I had been spreading lime down Ulpha way with David Birch and we stopped of at the Travellers Rest pub for a drink – though I doubt if the landlord would have been best pleased when he had seen the state of his carpet afterwards!

Spreading lime in those days was not for the faint hearted. Mr Woodhouse of Low Wray, Ambleside had land up Robin Lane, Troutbeck. The lane was very rough and was on very high ground – looking across to Wansfell. We had two tractors and spreaders, as this was a long way to cart from the wagon. We used the elevator to do the loading as this was burnt lime but later we used ramps. When it was really steep we would use the caterpillar tractor (or crawler) going straight up and down and the wheel tractor did all the lower land. We usually went up and down fifteen foot apart watching of course which way the wind was blowing.

It was hard work using the caterpillar tractors and the thing you hated most was throwing a track off. Sometimes you could get them back on by reversing, if not you had to jack them up, this meant carrying jacks and planks up the hillside. It was an awful job, as you sometimes had to dig down to get the jacks under, often in the rain and crawling about in mud.

The first time I drove a cater-pillar tractor was at Broughton Moor Slate Quarry and it was so steep that when you were coming down the hill you were looking onto the rooftops – it made my hair fair stand on end! Once when spreading lime at Grasmere it ran away through the wall and into the next field.

One day in 1957 we were spreading lime down the Ulverston area and it was a cold day and the farmer came out and the farmer's wife said, 'Bring them lads in for a cup of tea!' She

John Todd one of our workers spreading lime with the crawler (David Brown 50TD Caterpillar) just above the Jungle Café in late 1950s.

opened a cupboard and this mouse shot across the back and down. The farmer said, 'We will have to get rid of this mouse mother! Right 'o then.' She got this cheese down and where the mouse had been nibbling the

Some of the lads from M Croft's, Wildman Street. Pictured are Mick Braithwaite; Eric Burns; Alf Woof; Eric Worth and Sid Dixon. *Alf Woof*

cheese she cut if off and said, 'Here you are lads, a piece here for each of you!'

In January 1957 while spreading lime for Norman Postlethwaite, of Riddings Farm, Howgill, the bridge collapsed when the lime wagon was on it and it ended up in the river. We had to load the lime by hand (shovel) into the lime spreader and J. B. Hudson's of Sandside pulled out the wagon. The driver was Norman Forsythe and fortunately he wasn't hurt. As the lime was burnt lime a lot of the fish in the river died as the lime takes the oxygen out of the water.

We had another similar incident where we had a lot of hand shovelling. This time we were spreading lime at two big farms, Whinfell Park and Hornby Hall, near Temple Sowerby and owned by Mr Pollock. Hornby Hall had been an Air Force base during the Second World War. Both were large arable farms and that year I remember we put about six hundred tons of lime on the two farms. The lime was from Hartley Quarries at Kirkby Stephen and Derek Ousby for T. K. Robinson's and Bob Littlefair of Littlefairs haulage were the two hauliers. This day Bob's wagon ran off the road and tipped over – so we had a lot of shovelling to do before the breakdown lorry driven by Jim Carruthers from Skippers, Mintsfeet Estate, Kendal, came with a large winch to do the necessary.

A line up of Croft's Fordson tractors in Kendal Auction Mart in 1961. The first two are Power Majors and the other five are Dextas. Note the wooden sales hut from where business was done during market days. *Alf Woof/Westmorland Gazette*

One day in 1957–58 whilst spreading lime at Mr Cowperthwaite's farm up Gaisgill, near Tebay, he brought out a big 750 cc Harley Davidson motorbike, which had running boards instead of footrests, from an old shed. He started it up and let me have a ride on it – it was quite an experience to ride such a big beast.

One day at Bank House Farm, Barbon, the clutch on the tractor went. We brought a Salamander stove to keep warm while working on the tractor it was such a cold day. Alf Woof from Croft's fitted the new clutch.

Sometimes the lime would freeze in the wagons and it was an awful job to get it out. Tractors would freeze up on the road because there was no anti-freeze in, partly because it would have been a waste of time as they constantly leaked water and it would have been lost. Tractors as a rule were generally drained off at night

Tommy Duckett came to work for us in 1964 and stayed for three or four years doing general work. Tommy, dad and me built a lime spreader wagon, this was from a four-wheel drive Morris Commercial ex-War Department recovery vehicle and came from Dan Martindale's at Chorley. We put a lime spreader body on it and took out the original petrol engine, which was an old side-valve and replaced it with a 4D Ford diesel engine. Dad Christened it 'The Moke' and we used to also spread salt with it for Westmorland County Council round our area. The Moke lasted about four years doing both jobs – it was excellent while it lasted! I always enjoyed going to see Dan as he was quite a character wearing clogs and oily overalls. He always used to greet me saying, 'Come over here lad and see what thou thinks of this?'

On my way home from Coniston one day, I stopped of to see my Uncle Harry at Skelwith Bridge and left the tractor and spreader parked outside his house when I went in for a cup of tea. Only I had forgotten to set the handbrake and it ran into the next-door neighbour's wall. I didn't make that mistake again! I also had the job of rebuilding his wall.

Lime spreading, you see, was not always straightforward and you had to have your wits about you especially whilst spreading on steep land, as it could be dangerous. In the 1980s I overturned the tractor and spreader whilst on Troutbeck Park and John Woof from Kendal came with a tractor and winch and righted it for me and off I went to continue the job. The accident happened when I went into a hollow with the tractor and the full load of lime pulled us over.

Mavis and Lindsay outside her brother's flat in Romney Avenue, Kendal in the summer of 1961.

Using one of the flail hedgers at Wilson Garnett's farm at Ackenthwaite, near Milnthorpe in 1974.

IX

1960s

OUR DAUGHTER LINDSAY WAS BORN IN 1960 and attended both the old school in Natland and later the new one. She started school in 1965 and there were fifty pupils there then. The headmaster was Mr Hicks and Mrs Lund taught the younger ones. She had a fell pony called 'Robert.' Later she attended Longlands Girls School, Kendal, (now part of Queen Katherine School). She enjoyed sprinting and cross-country running and was a member of Cockermouth Amateur Sports Association and then joined the Kendal Athletics Association. She took a catering course at Kendal Technical College. Lindsay worked part-time at High Laverock House Hotel, where she met her husband Tim Mills, who worked at Spital Farm. They later moved to Armistead Hall, near Settle, where Tim was farm manager, and later to Knott End. Lindsay is now living in Natland with our two granddaughters Samantha and Rachel.

Back to work! We started doing hedges 1959–60. Hedge cutting began in August and carried on through to January. The hedge cutter had a cutter bar and then about 1974 flail hedge cutters came in and I bought one from R. Lloyds, Penrith. The advantage of these being the lack of cleaning up as it smashed up all the pieces. The first farm where I used a flail was Wilson Garnett's at Ackenthwaite. I remember the tractor rearing up as there wasn't enough ballast on the front. We covered a big area from Milnthorpe to Burton and Kendal, later on Grange-over-Sands, Cartmel and Flookburgh then to Field Broughton, Newby Bridge, Rusland Valley, Hawkshead, Sawrey, Cunsey, High & Low Wray and Windermere.

We were also fortunate to obtain the contract with British Waterways for cutting the grass and hedges along the canal banks from Stainton to Lancaster. The cutting was always delayed until November due to the wildlife, flower and fauna and would take me about five weeks to do. One day at Stainton a large hole appeared on the bank and the tractor went down as far as the axle and had to be pulled out with a tractor and winch. I was near Crooklands one day during a spell of hard frosty weather and the canal was frozen over and I saw a fox run across the ice. Quite a sight! Cutting along the edge of the canal one day near Lancaster the slabbing boards gave way and I ended up in the water. I was lucky not to have tipped over – it took three tractors to pull me out.

In 1962 Tom Ward came to Meathop Park and me and dad ploughed about a hundred acres for him. The land was very sandy but good to plough. He grew about eighty acres of barley and twenty acres of potatoes. In the spring down on the marsh it was very windy and cold with the wind blowing out of the east and all this land had been reclaimed during the war. A new sea wall was built in 1931. It was built during the depression years and it is said that business men from the cities arrived by train to Meathop Viaduct, dressed in their city suits and bowler hats to work on the wall!

The original sea wall was built in the 1860s and was called the Brogden Bank after one of the engineers. It had been breeched six times before building of the new wall in 1931. While ploughing in the spring-time you could not see for seagulls and the fine sand would blow and fill the ridges level.

A friend of mine, Frank Hartley, was a bank ranger at Meathop and Foulshaw and he was responsible for catching rabbit and moles, as their burrowing would weaken the bank. In 1967 the bank was washed out near Meathop Viaduct and nearby Bela Viaduct was knocked down.

There was a big freeze in Britain in 1962–63 and it froze hard for nearly three months. I used to go round the farms with my welder to thaw the pipes, so the cattle as well as humans could get water. The ice in some places was eight inches thick. I remember one day while spreading lime I was able to take a short cut across the frozen river.

When we were travelling on the road between jobs we used to get queues behind us and used to pull in where possible to let them past. Some people of course got annoyed and would give us the V-sign!

Combine harvesting was a very dusty job as there were no cabs in the early days. I would take the combine, a Massey Harris 780 combine, down to the Cartmel area and leave it there until we were finished. Every morning I had to go down and before I started cutting I had to grease up and sharpen the cutter bar knife and this would take about an hour, then when the dew came of it was ready to go.

Sometimes if there was no dew you could cut late at night with your lights on – these had to be fitted to early machines. In 1967 we bought another combine, a Claas Matador, a German make, dull green

Mr Croft (wearing glasses) and Mrs Croft hosting (invited farmers) the launch of the new Fordson Super Major at their premises in 1961. *Alf Woof/Westmorland Gazette*

in colour. This was a tanker and was a better machine whereby the barley was augured straight from the tank directly into a trailer with high sides. There was no need now for the combine to stop – the tractor and trailer would follow the harvester round when it was combining and at the same time it would be auguring out the barley into the high-sided trailer. My customers in the Cartmel area were: Ted Wilson – (Sandgate, Flookburgh); Alan Proctor – (Mireside); Michael Philipson – (Cannon Winder, Flookburgh); Alec Hornby – (Raven Winder), Edwin Morris – (Wraysholme Tower); Edwin Moor – (East Plain, Flookburgh); Jim Lowery – (Short Horn, Holker) and Henry Fearon – (Walton Hall, Cartmel). A lot of my customers became very good friends.

Mavis had quite a problem trying to estimate when we would be home for meals and trying to keep them warm. Sometimes I would phone her when I was going to be late, other times it was just not possible if I was a long way from a phone. She would even bring a meal out for us so that we could continue on into the evening. If we were there for a few days she would come in the car to pick me up. She also followed me in the car when we were moving machinery from one job to the other – this could sometimes be done the night before – setting it up and saving time next morning so we could get an early start. I have on occasion slept the night on the settee when I have come in after midnight and didn't want to disturb her. It was also very difficult during busy times to plan to go out anywhere – everybody wanted you at the same time when weather was good!

One wet day when there was no combining I went with Jim Benson the fisherman (from Flookburgh) for shrimps in his old Nuffield tractor and trailer. The fishermen use this make of tractor as they have a good ground clearance – driving miles out into the estuary. With the tide out Jim drove very fast out through the water that was sometimes two feet deep in areas and I would hang on for grim death as we went out towards Chapel Island, where once a monastery stood – this was some three miles from shore. We seemed to go out for a long time before returning with shrimps and white bait. It was quite an experience I have never forgotten – also a very cold and wet one as you can imagine!

Left: Demonstrating the new Ford Ransome two-furrow reversible plough and Fordson Super Dexta tractor at Low Rowell Farm, near Milnthorpe.
Standing second from left is Hugh Burton (salesman for Croft's) and his father Rob Burton from Field End, Docker. Further along – hatless is Alan Cowperthwaite (salesman) and standing next to tractor, wearing glasses is Mr Worth (manager). Also present are two demonstrators – on left and driving the tractor.
Alf Woof/Westmorland Gazette

Another farm I used to go to was East Plain and it had an old Air Force Camp nearby (Cark Aerodrome at Flookburgh) there are still some of the runways, two or three aeroplane hangers and a lot of shelters. A Spitfire landed there one day when I was working. The stone for the runways came from Broughton Moor Quarries. Today there is a large holiday camp there and the airport is still used for parachuting and car boot sales during the summer.

Over the years as well as Crofts we did quite a lot of business with P. V. Dobson at Levens. Dad used to buy of Percy and bought two Fordsons from him in 1949–50. We later dealt with Fred Scott and other members of the sales staff. They are a family firm and in the 1960s through until I finished I bought quite a lot of tractors from them including my last in 1996 that was a 398 Massey Ferguson – 4-wheel drive.

I remember in 1966 when we were spreading lime on the east side of the lake at Coniston when we heard the roar of a large jet engine starting up, this was Donald Campbell's 'Bluebird'. We saw it coming down the lake, what a sight it was. He only did one run that day.

Mum's cancer sadly came back in 1967 and she died in hospital at Kendal, on 22 June 1968. She was only fifty-eight. We missed her greatly. She had loved her little dog, a miniature Schnauzer, a German breed, grey/brown coloured and aptly named 'Rags.' Her favourite walks when we lived in Scarbrook were along the canal towards Natland or down to the river from Watercrook Farm. She loved Scotland and spent several holidays with dad there in the caravan. Her life had been taken up with keeping dad's books, her family, keeping house, gardening, painting, together with visiting friends and relations, especially her niece and husband, Winnie and Peter MacDiarmid, gamekeeper at Barbon Manor.

After mum died, dad did for himself for a while and had his meals with us. We had moved by this time into our new house at Ashgill, 61 Helmside Road, Oxenholme. Dad then had a housekeeper. When mum died Mavis took over the job of bookkeeping.

By 1969 dad had slowed down as he had developed a bad heart. He was told by the doctor to rest but he still just wanted to be out with the lads, either talking to them in the yard or coming out with one or two of his old mates to see what we were up to. He sadly died on 12 July 1972. I then had to decide which direction to take the business. I thought it through and came to the conclusion that hay time as we knew it was over and was being quickly overtaken by silage. At this time there was a lot of pipe track being laid and I was doing a lot of the reseeding work. I made the decision of just doing the cultivating side.

Hay time died a slow death and silage took over. I always found when we did hay that mowing and baling always used to clash and you were racing from job to job, dependant on the time of day. There was never of course enough hours in any one day. So in 1973 I had a sale and streamlined my business, I got rid of the mowing machines, balers and combine harvesters. After this my main work was ploughing, reseeding, hedge cutting and lime spreading.

I also had another couple of other lads working for me that I have not mentioned – Barry Cheeseman (April 1969–72) and John Woof (1970–72) both these did general contracting for me.

In 1973 I was approached by ICI with a view to taking on a contract for direct drilling. This was carried out in the summer months and was the process whereby the seed was drilled (input) directly into the sod/turf (save ploughing) with a special disc drill. The ground had to be first sprayed with Gramoxone beforehand and then left between 8-10 days for the grass to die. Crops that were drilled this way could be stubble turnips, kale, rape and grass seed. Mini slug pellets were also used. I took on the contract and my area covered Lancaster, Sedbergh, Kirkby Lonsdale, Ulverston and some work in West Cumberland. The good thing about direct drilling was that it did not poach (churn up) the land and was then mainly strip grazed. I did nearly eight hundred acres a year for them and this lasted for about twelve years before people went eventually back to the traditional system of ploughing and reseeding – it was found that better crops could be achieved. In the 1970s kale went out of favour as it was too labour intensive and farmers were beginning to keep more cows for milk and needed more grass and silage.

Keith Edmondson became a very good friend to me and visited our house quite a lot after his father died in 1968. Keith did quite a lot of jobs for me from time to time. In 1974 he went to the T. T. races (Tourist Trophy) in the Isle of Man with me, Bob Littlefair, Bob Coates and sailed from Liverpool. The weather was very good and we stayed for a week. There were the usual races for 125, 250, 500 and 750 cc. I remember we stood at Badon Bridge, a hump back bridge, where all the bikes and sidecars seemed to take off from – an excellent place for spectators to stand. We had a most enjoyable week.

In 1975 with regards to lime spreading I decided it would be more profitable if I took on the whole job and miss out the middleman, which is only good business sense. So I now bought the lime from the quarries (Magnesium Lime – Durham); Withers Lime – Carnforth; Holme Park – Burton; Stainton Quarries – near Barrow; Shap Beck – Harrison's,

103

formerly British Steel – this side of Shap). I arranged the haulage to the farm, though sometimes I did not have to do this as the quarries sometimes had their own wagons. We would spread the lime on the farms as we did before and bill the farmer for the whole thing, the one disadvantage being you had to lay out all the money to start with, so you had to know your customers well (they had to be good payers). Various people hauled lime for us – Les Brunskill at Shap; Hanleys – Crosby Garrett, near Kirkby Stephen – also had a lime store with Magnesium Lime in. Some were only small, only having the one wagon – Michael Dinsdale from Newbiggin Lune, and Tony Ritson from Appleby. David Birch of Lindale at that time had two or three wagons and George Bell from Gaisgill had two. All good little firms.

Lime was unloaded from the wagons by reversing them up a ramp and the spreader would be backed underneath. The tailboard was dropped and the wagon tipped up so the lime would slide out, somebody would stand at the back and give the relevant hand signal (up or down) when the spreader was full. You would get five or six loads from the big wagons, the spreaders held about three tons. The drivers were good lads generally and you could have a good crack and a bit of leg pulling – it all helped in these long days doing a long and dirty job!

Things of course have moved on from when I first started. Lime is not used as much now because of the expense and the way farming is now (not as profitable). At one time there used to be only – lime, ground limestone (milled), kibbled lime (good on old pasture land – burned it) magnesium lime that came from Durham – that helped prevent staggers in livestock and basic slag. Phosphates, potash and calcified seaweed (Cornwall) came in latterly – used to spread quite a bit of that. This used to come in granulated form – in 50-kilo (1 cwt) bags and now in half-ton bags. Some of the wagons now have their own loaders attached for loading and unloading these bags. In latter years when working we used to wear boiler suit, body-warmers, jeans, leggings and waterproof outer garments and scarf round your neck (to prevent dust getting down) and rubber gloves wintertime to try to prevent your fingers being covered in sores. Roll bars came out in 1970 and safety cabs became compulsory in 1972. Roll bars could be turned back to go into a low building on the farm. Tractors now have heaters in with spring-loaded seats for a comfortable ride and of course cabs that keep you dry with power steering

Right: Me in 1962 combining with a Massey Harris 780 combine harvester at Tony Gibson's, Ninezergh Farm, Levens. Barry Cheeseman (woolly hat) and Alan Hayton.
Joseph Hardman

Me in 1984 at Stephen Johnston's Farm at Speilbank Farm, Cartmel. Massey Ferguson 290 tractor and Atkinson Land Drive spreader. The wagon was Saunders from Spark Bridge, Greenodd and the lime came from nearby Stainton Quarry.

Busy spreading – bearing in mind wind direction!

and a radio to keep you company. Most of the tractors now are 4-wheel drive and are more versatile for most jobs. They do however come at a price, the 100 hp today will cost you up to £30,000 – that of course is with your deluxe cab and all the other luxuries of tractor driving in the 21st century! I wonder, what dad would have said?

Back again to days past. John Proctor whose father farmed at Spital Farm, Kendal was a distant relation of my father. John moved to Eskdale Green in West Cumberland in 1976 and I went to plough for him. We took the tractor and plough on a tipper wagon belonging to Geoff Packham of Carnforth. The route we took was via Broughton-in-Furness and over Birka Moor to Stanton Bridge. I spent a week there and I stayed in a pub at Drigg, next to the railway line and the bed shook every time a train went by. Meals were not so good, mostly tinned ham that was like rubber and the potatoes like bullets! I would have a drink at night and a good crack to the locals who were mostly workers at Sellafield. John grew potatoes, cabbages, lettuces and cauliflowers for the retail market. He also kept about twenty bullocks. It took me three and a half hours to drive home in the tractor and I was very pleased to be back home to Mavis and good homemade meals!

X

Vintage Tractors

IN 1970 I STARTED COLLECTING VINTAGE TRACTORS and the very first tractor I obtained was a Field Marshall from Mrs Armitage (nee Pumphrey) at Preston Patrick Hall Farm. It had been used for winching out hedges and trees in the early stages of the building of the M6 motorway and afterwards laid abandoned at the bottom of a steep bank. The tractor weighed a good three tons and it took two four-wheel drive tractors to pull it out. Water had been left in and this caused the cylinder head and engine block to crack. Our first job was to get these welded. Then when we had everything sorted and in working order, we gave it four coats of Field Marshall green paint (bedroom door just had two!). It had taken us six months to get it restored to rally condition. There was no documentation; we wanted an old number and had to register it with Swansea at the driving licence centre. It looked good and was in excellent working order when it was finished and we were chuffed to bits. My father and I were members of the Morecambe Bay Traction Engine Club and they held rallies at Levens Hall and we proudly took our tractor. We later joined the Cumbria Vintage Steam Club and with them took part in the 1974 Kendal Torchlight Procession which is held annually in the beginning of September.

That was just the start, I had got hooked on the idea of restoring even though I didn't really have the time. I then acquired a Massey Harris 744 that came from Sandworth, near Whitehaven and Bob Littlefair kindly went with me in his wagon and brought it back. I acquired an International Farmall M (American), this came from David Rigg who lived at Staveley. We had these tractors for quite a while and I was getting nowhere with them and they were taking up valuable space so sadly I sold them – the time was not there to be spent on them.

Time has gone on and since giving up work I have been able to restore the Rushton Hornsby stationary engine that John Whitwell gave me in 1974 (mentioned previously when it powered John's saw bench many

Left: Dad in 1971 with the Field Marshall we did up at Levens Hall.

years ago). I stripped it all down, cleaned all the parts and then painted them. The engine is beautifully made, down to the castings and the piston itself is about fourteen inches long by seven inches wide. I didn't dare take the piston rings off to clean, as I had no spares, so I cleaned out the grooves by turning them round. Next I rebuilt the engine and put a new water tank on for the cooling system, this held about twenty-five gallons of water, all the pipe work from the water tank to the engine was also renewed. Lastly I made a seven hundredweight trailer to transport it on. It had never really run for thirty-eight years so I rang Edward Baker (mechanic), Garths Farm, New Hutton and he came down to give me a hand to start it as he is an expert on stationary engines.

I asked Edward if he thought it would start and he said, 'That as long as you got a good spark on the magneto it would be okay.' So I cleaned the points thoroughly and it's spark 'would have knocked a donkey over!' We set up the magneto timing, put some petrol in the tank, Edward gave it three or four turns on the starting handle and it fired into life. As you can imagine I was very pleased with the way it ran – a blast straight out of the past!

I am now restoring a Fordson Super Dexter but my biggest problem so far is getting spares. After that my next project waiting to be done is a 1956 Fordson Major, deluxe model, diesel, with belt pulley lights and hour meter, registered number DJM 13, bought as new for £650 from Norman Crofts. I also know its complete history, it had been father's and used for threshing and lime spreading before being sold to Jimmy Lancaster at Prizet Farm, in 1968. In January 2004 I proudly bought it back from them and it is now back home waiting to be lovingly restored to what it was like all those years ago when it was first bought – and of course full of memories!

I have quite a few other vehicles waiting in the yard to be done. Another tractor, this time a 1949 Ferguson Continental, six-volt straight petrol, that once belonged to Hughie Tatham, from Windermere. I have also two motorbikes awaiting the same treatment – AJS 350 (1953) and a Yamaha Enduro (1975) from Witherslack. So plenty to keep me busy!

XI

The writing was on the Wall

IN OCTOBER 1986 KEITH ROWEND of Stool End Farm, Great Langdale, rang to ask if I wanted to take part in an advertisement for Harvey's Sherry. The advert was to depict a ploughman's lunch and I was to plough a piece of land at Stool End. It was a very interesting day working with the cameramen getting the right light etc – besides being well paid for it! Fame at last!

For a couple of years then my health had been deteriorating, some days I could hardly get on my tractor. If I sat down I went to sleep. One morning in 1989 I was driving to a job I was doing for John Bethel at Bowness when I came across a lady trying to start her car. I stopped to render assistance and offered to push her car. On returning to my pick-up I felt both dizzy and short of breath. One of John's men, Bill Johnston, who had been travelling in front of me had turned back to see where I was. He took me home and Mavis phoned the doctor. After a brief examination she told me briefly that she thought that the main heart valve had narrowed but required tests to find out for sure what exactly was wrong.

I next saw Mr Brown, a consultant at Westmorland General Hospital. Ultra sound readings confirmed that the aorta was very narrow and my mitral valve was leaky. Next I went to see a cardiologist at Wythenshawe Hospital, Manchester. More tests were done and I was informed that surgery was required to replace the valve with a Teflon one. In layman's terms 'we need to do a good plumbing job!' At that time there was a twelve months waiting list and this was June. They then told me not to book a holiday. Don't know what happened to the waiting list but I did not have long to wait, by August I was back at Wythenshawe for the operation. That morning I was prepared (pre-med), anaesthetised and went down to theatre, only to be returned to the ward. It had to be cancelled as a large fire in the city had caused power failure. I was sent home for a week to recover from the anaesthetic.

Me busy ploughing with a Kverneland plough and Massey Ferguson 398 at Jenkin Cragg Farm, near Benson Knot in 1990.

On the Green, Mrs Johnstone, Pearson Charnley – who went with me on our train journey and Miss Snowball planting a commemorative tree to celebrate the Queen's Silver Jubilee in 1977.

I returned a week later and this time the operation went ahead without any more hiccups. It was successful and I went home ten days later with my new St Jude's valve. All valves are registered for safety reasons Mr Brown said, 'It should be easy to remember, just think of the popular Beatles album 'Heh Jude!'

When I was recuperating I managed to fit in taking a train journey I had always wanted to do up the west coast. So this day, Mavis kindly took me, Pearson Charnley and Tony Bland to Oxenholme Railway Station to catch the train to Carlisle. From there we went down the coast to Sellafield, a coach took us to the Visitors Centre to have a look round. After that we caught the train down to Barrow then via Lancaster back to Oxenholme and home again. There was some mutterings of 'Last of the Summer Wine' was never in it!' We had a great day! Pearson sadly died in 2003 and a commemorative bench was placed on the Green in recognition of all the work he did for the village of Natland and the new development of houses now being built is called 'Charnley Fold'.

Anyway after three months I was allowed to do some light work – so I did some hedge cutting! I owe a big debt of gratitude to two very good lads – John Holmes (who I had taken on to cover for my illness) and David Guy (who had worked with me from 1985) who had kept the business going during my absence.

In the 1990s during the winter I used to do the snow ploughing at Asda, Great Mills (now Focus) and Natland School. I had a rear mounted snow plough and would go down at 6 am using my own discretion and remove the snow or spread salt on if very slippy using a lime spreader.

I continued work until 2002 when my health again deteriorated and the doctor told me in no uncertain terms that I would have to finish. This was the end of the chapter for me. David Guy, who had worked for me for some time, took over some of the business and bought the machinery he needed for hedge cutting, tractor ploughing and cultivating. Eddie Hottersall from Ingleton bought the lime spreader and ramps. Bob Littlefair and me got the rest of the machinery, bits and pieces, ready for sale at Kendal Auction Mart. As you can imagine it was a very sad time for me, it was a business I had worked for nearly fifty years. It was so much part of my life and my father's before me.

My girls - Rachel, Samantha and Lindsay outside our new bungalow.

Busy tinkering in my work shed!

XII

Retirement

RETIREMENT TAKES A BIT OF GETTING USED TO but I keep myself busy doing jobs around the house which we built in 2001. I built this bungalow next to our original one and this is called 'Sonora' after a place we liked in California. It is our pride and joy. I still have a workshop with a solid fuel stove – so I enjoy working in relative comfort doing up tractors and engines. I also like to walk everyday if I can, usually do about two or three miles. My favourite walks are down by the river north to Low Mills or south to Sedgwick. Friday afternoons I can be found in the village hall playing short mat bowls. I have now more time to enjoy going out with Mavis and seeing more of my daughter Lindsay and our two granddaughters, Samantha and Rachel. I like visiting people and friends that I have made during the years and Sundays usually finds me up at Billy Kitchen's at Hawes Farm just down the lane.

When I was working I never had time for holidays – the first I ever had was in the Orkneys in the early 1990s. Things have of course changed and in 1999 I was persuaded to go to California with Mavis, Lindsay, Samantha and Rachel. We had a very interesting time visiting L.A., Las Vegas and San Francisco. It made me realise what I had been missing and I now have time to go away whenever we want. I have been back to America for the Mardi Gras in New Orleans, visiting Memphis, Nashville and Gracelands. Italy is another favourite place and last year we went to Canada, Germany and Prague. The world's my oyster!

I still enjoy going to farm sales and being able to keep in touch with people and how things are progressing – that way of life never leaves you. I have time now to go to ploughing matches with Jimmy Lancaster. I still miss though getting up early in a spring morning and ploughing – turning over that very first piece of turf. Uncovering the freshly coloured piece of soil that you have been responsible in bringing to the surface, it is quite beautiful and it has a smell (aroma) all of its own. You are surrounded by wildlife – the seagulls fly in and surround you as you work, as well as others, crows, oystercatchers, lapwings, curlews and birds of the hedgerow. The wild animals caught off their guard sleeping or play-ing – rabbits, hares (more or less gone), deer and the odd badger. All this is so much a part of country life together with being out in all weathers no matter the season of the year.

Life has been good, I have enjoyed my working life, the area I was born and brought up in – never moved far – just over a mile! Never wished to go any further or wanted to until these last few years – after perhaps a little persuasion though I am not complaining. It probably helps to rein-force how lucky I have been to have lived and worked in such a beautiful area.

I have always enjoyed working with machinery, tinkering with it, learning how to fix it, clean it up – bringing these old bits of machinery back to life. I have a lot to be thankful for and would gladly do it all again. Now I have time to do things more slowly instead of rushing about at all hours, to enjoy my family, holidays and my beloved tractors – even got myself a white MGB sports car that I am doing up (for Mavis suppos-edly!) and will take to the lanes this summer and visit the friends where once I had worked. With all probability I will acquire one or two more machines along the way to put round the back to do up on a rainy day – and join the queue already waiting to be done!

Me in Scotland enjoying retired life to the full!

If you have enjoyed this book you may also enjoy other books
published by Helm Press.

'*A Westmorland Shepherd*' His life, poems and songs

'*Elephants On The Line*' Tales of a Cumbrian Railwayman

'*Dear Mr Salvin*' The story of the building of a 19th century
Ulverston church

'*All In A Lifetime*' The story of a Dalesman as told to June Fisher

'*Hawkshead Revisited* A Walk in time through Hawkshead

'*A Century of Heversham and Leasgill*' A walk in time through
these old Westmorland villages

'*An Old Westmorland Garage*' The story behind Crabtree's of
Kendal

'*Ambleside Remembered*' People and Places, Past and Present

'*Snagging Turnips and Scaling Muck*' The Women's Land Army in
Westmorland

'*The Windermere Ferry*' History, Boats, Ferrymen & Passengers

'*Kendal Green*' A Georgian Wasteland Transformed

'*Kendal Brown*' The History of Kendal's Tobacco & Snuff Industry

'*On & Off the Rails*' The Life of a Westmorland Railwayman

'*Stainton. An Old Westmorland Parish*' Reminiscences of a local farmer

H E L M
P R E S S
10 Abbey Gardens, Natland, Kendal, Cumbria LA9 7SP
Tel: 015395 61321
E-mail: HelmPress@natland.freeserve.co.uk
www.natland.freeserve.co.uk